2017 EDITION

iPad®

MADE EASY

This is a FLAME TREE book
First published 2016

Publisher and Creative Director: Nick Wells
Project Editor: Polly Prior
Art Director: Mike Spender
Layout Design: Jane Ashley
Copy Editor: Daniela Nava
Technical Editor: Mark Mayne
Screenshots: Roger Laing
Thanks to: Josie Mitchell, Laura Bulbeck, Esme Chapman, Emma Chafer,
Stephen Feather and Karen Fitzpatrick

This edition published 2016 by
FLAME TREE PUBLISHING
6 Melbray Mews
Fulham, London SW6 3NS
United Kingdom

www.flametreepublishing.com

18 20 19 17
3 5 7 9 10 8 6 4

ISBN 978-1-78664-086-4

A CIP record for this book is available from the British Library upon request.

Printed in China

2017 EDITION

iPad®

MADE EASY

ROGER LAING

FLAME TREE
PUBLISHING

CONTENTS

Time to get familiar with the iPad, its controls, all the essential apps you'll need and the everyday tasks that you'll use it for. Starting with the basics, you will learn all about the iPad's anatomy and the whereabouts of different buttons, as well as understanding what goes on inside your device. This chapter also takes you through other essentials such as using the App Store and syncing.

The iPad is the whole world at your fingertips. In this chapter you'll learn how to browse the internet, send and receive messages and emails, use video calling, and master social media channels such as Facebook and Twitter. Getting connected doesn't end there; you'll also get to grips with how to make the most of the iPad's location services.

With its high quality Camera and Video apps, the iPad is the perfect tool when it comes to capturing, viewing and storing great photos and movies. Featuring step by step guides to taking, editing, and sharing photos and videos, this chapter will leave you feeling like a fully competent iPad photographer. In addition you'll learn how to rent and buy videos through the iTunes store, and view them using Apple TV.

The iPad is the perfect device for browsing, downloading, arranging and reading books and magazines via the iBooks app – and this chapter shows you exactly how to do so. What's more this chapter introduces other reading apps such as Kindle and Zinio, and details how to adjust the appearance of text to ensure that you get the best reading experience possible.

When it comes to finding a comprehensive entertainment device, the iPad is king. This chapter describes how the iTunes, Podcast and Music apps allow you to use your iPad to browse, create and edit playlists and to make and share your own music. In addition you'll learn all about gaming on your iPad and discover apps that complement every aspect of your lifestyle, from shopping to cooking.

WORKING **184**

From built in apps such as Notes, to iWork productivity apps like Pages and Keynote, which can be downloaded from the app store, the iPad is your hub for work and play. This chapter will talk you through these vital apps, as well as apps for blogging and drawing. You will also learn how to print from your iPad and keep in the loop by using Calendar to schedule meetings and Contacts to stay in touch.

ADVANCED iPAD. **216**

Once you're comfortable with your iPad and know how to use it, it's time to really make it your own. This chapter tells you how to customize the way different apps and controls work. Amongst other things you will also learn how to troubleshoot issues such as connectivity and power loss, as well as introducing the various ways in which you can accessorize your iPad to optimum effect.

INTRODUCTION

Loved, desired and applauded since it was first launched, the iPad has revolutionized personal computing. Forget your laptop, ditch the desktop PC: the iPad is rapidly becoming the essential accessory for managing everyday life.

Above: The Retina display on the iPad offers incredible screen clarity, ideal for viewing video.

YOUR WORLD AT YOUR FINGERTIPS

The iPad is far more than a gadget. Once you have one it is almost impossible to remember life without it. Never before has there been a device that makes it this simple to read books, newspapers and magazines, browse the web, go shopping, play games, see movies, watch TV, listen to music, share photos, research ideas for business, write a report and organize the day. What's more, you can do all this and still communicate via email or chat with friends, family and work colleagues, whether close to home or across continents. With the iPad, your world is in your hand.

EVERYTHING YOU NEED TO KNOW

Apple is renowned for the simple elegance of their design. Following the principles set by their founder – the late Steve Jobs – they want to create technology that just works. While the iPad is user friendly, there is so much that it does that is not immediately obvious.

This book is designed to help you get the most from your iPad. It will guide you through the myriad ways you can use the iPad for both personal and business use. Like the iPad, we'll aim to make things simple and clear. Where it is unavoidable to use technical terms we will explain exactly what they mean.

Different Generations, Similar Features

Amazingly, since it first appeared in 2010, Apple has launched 12 different models of iPad, each with two options available – Wi-Fi only and Wi-Fi plus Cellular.

Above: The iPad home screen displays all your apps simply and clearly.

Unfortunately, the naming of each model has been confusing. The original iPad was clear and so was iPad 2. But that was followed not by iPad 3 but the New iPad featuring the super-high-resolution Retina display, which Apple dubbed 'Resolutionary'. The new iPad was itself replaced within six months by a faster version referred to as iPad with Retina display. After that came the iPad Air (to reflect its lightness) followed by the iPad Air 2. In addition, there have been four versions of the smaller iPad named iPad mini.

Now Apple has released a new series: the iPad Pro in two sizes. The larger 12.9" Retina display and optional Smart Keyboard is seen as a potential replacement for the laptop. Its little brother, the smaller 9.7" iPad Pro has significantly better cameras.

Above: The iPad mini is a smaller version of the iPad.

While there are physical differences between the different models – for example, iPad Pro has a more powerful processor than the others, and the original iPad has no camera – many features are controlled by the operating system (iOS). The latest iOS runs on all iPads, with the exception of the original iPad, but that still supports most features mentioned in this book. Where features are available only on specific models, this will be noted in the text.

SHORT SECTIONS

Pick up your iPad and flick through the screens and you'll often come across something new. Similarly, this book is not designed to be read in one sitting but to be a handy guide. For example, the section on gestures can be read on its own and you can practise them on your iPad until you feel confident that you can use them correctly. At the same time, it is a useful reference, if you need to remind yourself of some of the more advanced gestures later on.

STEP-BY-STEP

Throughout this book you'll find there are many step-by-step guides that take you through the precise actions you need to follow on certain tasks. This may be anything from connecting to your wireless network, setting up email or editing your photos to creating a new playlist for your music or troubleshooting app problems. Each step-by-step guide has clear, concise instructions on what to do and also explains any differences between the various iPad versions, so you can be sure you won't miss out.

HELP!

In the unlikely event you do get really stuck on a particular topic, we're here to help. Simply email your query to Flame Tree Publishing at *info@flametreepublishing.com*. While we cannot operate a 24-hour helpline for any iPad questions, we will respond by email as soon as possible.

YOUR GUIDE

If this is your first iPad, this book is designed to get you up and running as quickly as possible. There's plenty too for the more experienced user to discover. The author Roger Laing delves into some of the more advanced features and uses his experience as a technology writer to explain briefly and clearly how they improve your iPad experience and add to the fun.

Above: Editing photos is just one of the ways you can use your iPad.

DO MORE

Everyone has their own opinion on what's best about the iPad. It may be watching a movie or TV programme on a display that can vie with the best of screens. It could be playing games with a speed and power that rivals any console. It may be having a photo gallery to share with family and friends or the incredible range of apps, many of which have the potential to change the way you live and work. The good thing is you don't have to choose between any of these. The iPad has them all and more. This book will get you started; after that the possibilities are virtually unlimited.

Above: It is easy to use your iPad to watch films and TV programmes on websites such as BBC iPlayer.

SEVEN CHAPTERS

The contents of this book are split into seven chapters. Chapter one will show you how to get started with the iPad itself and the hundreds of thousands of apps available. Chapter two covers getting connected with email, video calling, social media and the like. Chapter three is all about photos and video – taking photos, editing them to add stunning effects, as well as viewing, storing and sharing them. It also offers practical advice on taking, viewing and editing your own videos, as well as buying and renting movies, and TV shows, etc. Chapter four is where to read all about the books, newspapers and magazines that turn your iPad into a digital reader. Chapter five is the entertainment channel, where you can discover how to listen, store and even make your own music or enter another world with games. Chapter six shows that the iPad is also a good work tool, which can help you organize your documents, your time, your contacts – in fact as much of your life as you allow. Chapter seven looks at the more advanced features that keep your iPad running smoothly – from customizing and setting your preferences to troubleshooting and security.

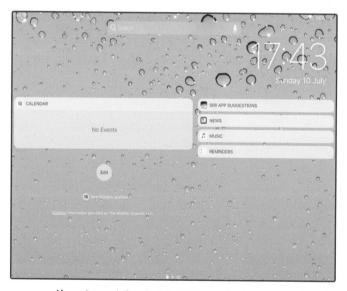

Above: Swipe right from the lock screen in iOS 10 and you have an enhanced Today page with the latest news, weather, calendar info and other notifications.

Above: Head to the App Store to browse and download apps and get the most out of your iPad.

HOT TIPS AND SHORT CUTS

Look out, throughout the book, for the Hot Tips, which provide quick and handy information on the way to get the best from your iPad. They also highlight many short cuts and quick techniques to help you become an expert iPad user.

APPTASTIC

Here in one handy list are the 100 essential apps that no iPad user will want to be without. They are linked to the relevant section in the book, so it's easy to refer back and get more information on the category they cover.

GETTING STARTED

WHAT IS AN iPAD?

Think of your iPad as the ultimate portable computer – light enough to take wherever you go, yet powerful and versatile enough to do whatever you need.

TABLET COMPUTER

The arrival of the iPad established the popularity of tablet computers, a type of mobile computer that typically has a touch screen rather than a normal keyboard. Previously, several computer manufacturers had launched tablets but they failed to take off. Apple succeeded because they believed the tablet, which is bigger than a smartphone but smaller than a laptop, had to be better than either at key tasks – such as displaying text and video, organizing your work life and brightening up your personal life.

YOUR ENTERTAINMENT CENTRE

Whether it's a long read, listening to your favourite music, playing a game with friends around the world or sharing a memory of good times with your photos, the iPad does it all.

Books and Periodicals

Your portable library, the iPad is an ebook reader which can store hundreds of texts inside and also

Above: Download, store and read hundreds of book and magazine texts on your iPad.

Hot Tip

The small software programs that run on the iPad are called apps (mini-applications). Apple has approved more than a million apps for download through the App Store.

Above: Use the touch screen controls in the iPad video app to view high definition music videos in full screen mode.

lets you buy more on the device. Apple has one app, iBooks, for reading and storing books. With many other apps from bookstores, magazines, newspapers and publishers, such as Amazon, you literally have access to millions of book titles worldwide and hundreds of periodicals.

Video

As video viewing is a key feature of the iPad, it comes with its own app. Click on the Videos icon and you can choose between viewing movies, TV shows or music videos, or go to the online store to see what's available to purchase.

Once you've started the video player, using the touch screen controls, you can view the video full screen for uninterrupted viewing. Not surprisingly, the app takes full advantage of the super clear Retina display available on all current models and can playback full HD video.

Music

Previously, the music app was named the iPod; now it takes full advantage of the iPad's larger screen and is more like iTunes that runs on your computer. The artists, for example, and their various album covers are shown on a grid. Select one and you can see all the tracks and associated album covers that you have by that artist.

Games

Games are another area where the iPad scores over the smaller screen iPhone. There are many games specially developed for the iPad, which has the speed and power to match the graphics of traditional games consoles. If you want to rank your scores against friends and family, sign up for an account on the iPad's Game Center app.

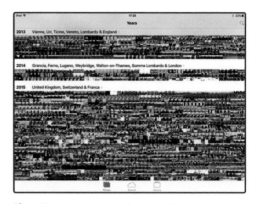

Above: Photos organizes your photos and videos according to where and when they were taken.

Photos

Open the Photos app and see all the digital photos stored in your iCloud Photo Library, which keeps all your snaps up-to-date across all your Apple devices. To save space, your photos and videos can be stored at a smaller size on the iPad with the original, full resolution versions on iCloud. To turn on this feature go to Settings, select iCloud, then Photos and select Optimise iPad Storage.

Photos is where you'll see the images you've taken with the camera (on all iPads except iPad 1). Flick through your pictures by swiping your finger across the screen.

Your photos and videos are automatically organized by where and when they were taken. Years groups together all the photos taken each year. Tap to open Collections, where the photos are arranged by the place where they were taken (such as a French holiday) and tap again to open Moments, which groups together pictures taken around the same time and place (like an afternoon on the beach).

Hot Tip

You get 5GB of free storage for your photos in iCloud and as your picture library grows you have the option to buy up to 1TB of storage.

YOUR BUSINESS RESEARCH ASSISTANT

The iPad is a wonderful research tool that can help you find the important information you need, take notes or even full reports and share them afterwards.

Web Content

With Safari for iPad you have a browser that is similar to any you have used on a computer. It gives you access to all the same research sources – from Google search to Wikipedia and millions in between. With support for tabbed browsing, it's now easy to move backwards and forwards between the different pages you have visited.

Making and Storing Notes

Nothing is worse than having an idea you want to make a note of and no way to write it down. Fortunately, the iPad comes with its own Notes app. Use the notepad to jot down ideas, plan a project and write down a meeting report. For writing a To Do list, the better option is the iPad's list writing app, called Reminders. This lets you create a task list – from the weekly shop to packing for a holiday – for which you can set a reminder that will alert you when it needs to be done.

Sharing Information

Your notes and reminders can be synced with your other Apple devices, so you always have the latest version. You can also share your reminders with others through iCloud. Similarly, there are many file sharing services – from Dropbox to Evernote and Google Docs – which enable you to collaborate and work on documents with friends and colleagues, wherever they are, direct from your iPad.

Above: Reminders allows you to make lists and set timed reminders. Sync your reminders with other Apple devices and share over iCloud to keep all relevant people updated, wherever they may be.

ANATOMY OF AN iPAD

While there are few obvious physical differences between iPads, there are some subtle and not so subtle variations between each generation. Here's your guide to the physical layout of the iPad.

FRONT

1 Headphone Socket

The 3.5 mm audio jack point works fine with headphones or earbuds you use with other Apple devices, such as the iPhone or iPod Touch, but others may need an inexpensive adapter to fit.

2 Sleep/Wake Button

Also known as the On/Off button.

○ **Sleep mode**: press this button once and this will put your iPad to sleep. You can still play music but the screen will be off. To wake the iPad instantly and start using it, press the Sleep/Wake button once (or the Home button) and swipe across the slide to unlock button.

○ **Shutdown**: turns the iPad off completely, saving your battery. To switch off, press and hold the Sleep/Wake button for a few seconds. Confirm your decision by using the slide to power off button to shut down.

Headphone socket **1**   FaceTime camera **3**   Sleep/wake button **2**

Home screen **4**

Display **7**

Retina display **8**

iPad dock **5**

6 Home button

❸ FaceTime Camera

As its name suggests, it is mainly meant for using with FaceTime video chat, so other people can see you. On current models the front camera supports 1.2-megapixel stills (5-megapixel stills on the smaller iPad Pro) and 720 HD (High-Definition) video.

❹ Home Screen

The Home screen has the app icons that you tap to run the app. Swipe right on the Home screen and you'll flip through the different pages of apps you have available. You can also organize your apps into folders. To do so, just press on an app icon until it starts shaking and then drag it on top of the icon you want to share the folder. A folder is automatically created, which you can rename. Tap on the folder and you can access the apps inside.

❺ iPad Dock

This dock bar appears at the foot of the Home screen and stays in place as you scroll between the pages. It means these apps are always available from any Home screen page. As a result you will want the apps you use most frequently to be in the dock. By default, the Safari, Mail, Photos and Music apps will be there, but you can customize the dock to include six apps of your choice. To add an app, press and hold until it begins to shake, then drag it to the dock. To make room for a different app, if you already have six in the dock, press and hold one of the apps then drag it to the Home screen.

❻ Home Button

The only physical button on the front of your iPad. When you are in an app press this once to return to the Home screen. Pressing it twice reveals the apps that are running. On newer iPads, the Home button has a fingerprint sensor for Touch ID, a security feature that lets you unlock your iPad using your thumb or finger.

Hot Tip

One way to help preserve battery life is to set your screen to Auto-Lock when you're not using it. To do so, tap the Settings icon, select General, then Auto-Lock and set the interval to the time you prefer.

❼ Display: iPad 1, 2 and Mini (*see* previous page)

The screen of the iPad 1 and 2 is 9.7 inches when measured diagonally with a resolution of 1024x768 pixels. The iPad mini shares the same resolution as its bigger siblings, but with a smaller display at 7.9 inches measured across the diagonal. On both screens, the backlit multi-touch display has a special coating to help prevent smearing and smudges.

❽ Retina Display: iPad 3, 4; iPad mini 2, 3, 4; iPad Air, iPad Air 2 and iPad Pro series (*see* previous page)

The Retina displays on these iPads means they can play movies in full HD. In fact, everything from video to photos and text is sharper and more detailed. The name Retina comes from the fact that with a pixel density of 264 pixels per inch (PPI) – 326 ppi for the iPad mini 2 and 4 – the pixels are too close together for a human eye to discern between them. The iPad Pro has the largest screen – 12.9", compared with 9.7" for the traditional iPads and smaller iPad Pro and 7.9" for the iPad mini series.

Touch screen

You control the machine and enter text by tapping and swiping the display. In addition, the iPad Pro has a connection for an optional smart Keyboard or you can use a digital stylus called Apple Pencil on the Touch screen.

REAR

❶ iSight Camera

The video camera on the iPad 2 (iPad 1 has no cameras) has a 0.7-megapixel lens that shoots video at 720p. Then came the 5-megapixel lens on later models, with 8-megapixels on the iPad Pro, iPad Air 2 and iPad mini 4, all shooting full

❶ iSight camera

❻ Side switch

❺ Volume buttons

iPad

❷ SIM card slot

❹ Speakers ❸ Lightning connector

1080p HD video. The 9.7" iPad Pro has a 12-megapixel lens and can shoot 4K HD Video. The full range of features includes video stabilization, auto-focus, tap to focus and face detection.

❷ SIM Card Slot

This holds the Nano-SIM card your telecommunications company will give you to access their data networks. The cover is easily removed using the SIM card tool supplied or an ordinary paper clip. Your iPad can connect to the regular 3G or faster 3.5G HSPA+ network and, in countries where they are available, the 4G LTE networks. The 9.7" iPad Pro has an embedded Apple SIM which allows you to connect to data plans on selected cellular networks direct from the iPad itself.

❸ Lightning Connector

To much consternation, the original 30-pin dock connector used with iPad 1, 2 and 3 was changed to the much lighter, smaller Lightning connector on later models. The dock connector allows you to hook up to your computer, power charger, camera connector and other accessories.

❹ Speakers

The speaker grills are at the bottom edge of your iPad, so make sure that they are not obscured by the cover you use.

❺ Volume Buttons

With the rocker button, you press one end to turn the sound up and the other to turn it down. As you adjust the setting, a box will appear on screen with a speaker icon and a volume strength bar.

❻ Side Switch

This can do one of two things. By default, it is used to lock the orientation of the iPad, so it stays in either vertical (portrait) or horizontal (landscape) mode. If you go to Settings, you can change it to be a mute switch that turns the iPad's volume off.

> ## Hot Tip
>
> Cleverly, the iPad remembers two volume settings: one for the volume you set when using headphones and the other for the sound level when using the speaker.

INSIDE THE iPAD

With each new model the iPad has become faster and more capable. Here we look at the main features to help you decide which one is right for you.

Memory (RAM)

As each new generation of iPad does more, so more memory is needed to run the operating system and apps. The

Above: The iPad unpacked! Complex and sleek, the iPad is also surprisingly environmentally friendly, boasting many eco features, including a recyclable aluminium and glass enclosure.

initial 256MB of memory has now increased to 1GB on the iPad mini 2 and iPad Air, 2GB for iPad mini 4, iPad Air 2 and 9.7" iPad Pro and 4GB for the 12.9" iPad Pro.

Processor

Each generation of the iPad has seen an increase in the power of the processor. The iPad Pro series and iPad Air 2 have tri-core processors, which means they can run up to 2.5 times faster and process graphics up to 5 times faster than the iPad Air. With faster processors and more memory, the top end iPads can take advantage of new features in the iOS and smoothly open two apps on the screen at the same time.

Storage Options

However much space you need to store your music, videos and photos, you'll probably end up wanting more. Each iPad series has different sizes ranging from 16GB, 32GB, 64GB and 128GB to 256GB. Typically, this would allow you to store:

- **16 GB**: 2,000 songs, 7,000 photos, 22 hours of video

- **32 GB**: 4,000 songs, 14,000 photos, 42 hours of video

- **64 GB**: 9,000 songs, 28,000 photos, 86 hours of video

- **128GB**: 18,000 songs, 56,000 photos, 170 hours of video

- **256GB**: 32,000 songs, 110,000 photos, 310 hours of video

Hot Tip

Don't forget to allow space to accommodate the larger file sizes of HD games and movies and high-resolution (hi-res) photos you may want to view on the Retina display.

Rather than carry everything around with you, you can use online storage services, such as Apple's iCloud, for your music, files and apps, downloading them only when you want them. However, that may not always be convenient. Downloads can be costly on 3G and you may not always have Wi-Fi access when you need it.

Wi-Fi/Cellular
All versions of the iPad are available with just Wi-Fi or with Wi-Fi plus Cellular. With a SIM card and subscription from a mobile provider, you can use their data networks to surf the web, download apps, get email, etc. No voice services are included on any iPad models, so you can't make a call as you can with the iPhone (except over Wi-Fi through services such as Skype and FaceTime).

High-speed Cellular
The latest iPad cellular models support 4G LTE (4G is the fourth generation of mobile networks: LTE, or Long Term Evolution, is a type of 4G technology). Currently, 4G coverage varies, but most countries have plans to roll out the technology, or a version of it, over the next couple of years. Check with your provider if your local version works with the iPad. 4G promises speeds about five times faster than existing 3G services. However, the latest iPads also include support for the faster 3G wireless technologies, such as HSPA+.

Bluetooth

Bluetooth is the wireless technology that lets you swap data quickly over short distances. The latest version 4.2 is faster and uses less power. It will still work with your existing Bluetooth accessories, such as wireless keyboards, photo uploaders, etc. However, you'll only get the full benefit of its energy efficiency if your devices support the new standard.

Smart Cover

The clever magnetic system of the Smart Cover switches your iPad on when you lift the cover and puts it to sleep when you close it.

Battery Life

Despite differences in screen resolution and processor power, battery life is the same across all iPads. That is: about 10 hours of power if used with Wi-Fi.

Above:
The Smart Cover, as well as waking, sleeping and protecting your iPad, is also a handy stand for reading, watching and typing.

Above: The main lock screen appears in iOS 10 as soon as you pick up your iPad. To unlock it, you now press the physical Home button.

Hot Tip

In practice, battery life greatly depends on how you use the iPad. You can help the power to last longer by adjusting screen brightness and reducing, or turning off, notifications, location services and push email.

iPAD BASICS

Getting started with your iPad is simple and opens up a whole new world of entertainment, communication and fun.

SET UP YOUR iPAD

When you get your brand new iPad, there's remarkably little in the box: just the iPad, power cord and not much else. There's no manual, which is one reason why this book can help to get your iPad adventures off to the best start.

Step-by-step

With earlier iPads you had to connect your iPad to your computer – and iTunes – to start the activation process. Since iOS 5.0 you can get going using Wi-Fi.

1. A brand new iPad comes partly charged, so you can start straight away. Turn it on by pressing the Sleep/Wake button on the top (the Apple logo will appear) and slide the button across to start.

2. Pick the language you want to use, by tapping on it. A blue tick will appear beside it. Tap the blue arrow to continue.

3. Choose your location from the list under the map. Usually, your country will be showing automatically. If not, tap Show More, pick your location and tap Next.

Above: Part of the iPad set up process asks you to select the language you want to use.

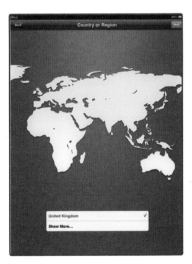

Step 3: Choose your location by selecting the country you live in from the list under the map.

4. Next, you'll be asked to connect to your Wi-Fi network. A list will open of those available. A lock beside a name shows it is secured and you will need a password to use it. Tap on your chosen network name. Alternatively, you can use your mobile connection.

5. You may want to share your location through mapping and social media apps. To do so, you'll have to turn Location Services on. Tap Enable Location Services here and then tap Next.

6. The usual terms and conditions appear for you to agree before you can proceed.

Step 5: Turn on Location Services to share your location through mapping and social media apps.

Step 6: Choose whether you want to set up your device as a new iPad or transfer data from an old iPad.

7. Now, it's time to activate your iPad. If this is your first iPad, select Set Up as New iPad and click the Next button in the top right hand corner. If you are transferring your data from a previous iPad, select one of the other options to transfer from iCloud or iTunes.

Step 8: Set up an Apple ID, or sign in with an existing Apple ID, so that you can download apps from App Store and access iTunes.

8. To get the most from your iPad, you need an Apple ID, which is also used to set up your iTunes account. Click Sign In with an Apple ID if you already have one. Otherwise, Create a Free Apple ID takes you through the process.

9. Apple then offers to turn on various features. Among them are iCloud, using iCloud for backup, and activating Find My iPad in case you lose your tablet.

10. A list of the phone numbers and email addresses on which you can be contacted via iMessage and FaceTime are shown. You can also set up Siri as your voice activated assistant and on later models register your fingerprint for unlocking your iPad using Touch ID. Go through a few more screens, including registration of your new iPad, and press the final button to Start Using iPad.

Step 9: iCloud is an extremely useful way of storing, backing up and sharing data across different devices.

If you are unsure, during setup, whether you want to activate any services offered, follow the link at the bottom of the screen, which explains more about them.

Mobile Connections

If you have a cellular iPad, you will need to install the SIM card, provided separately by the mobile network company. Simply open the SIM card holder on the side of the iPad – using the pin provided – and put in the SIM card. Turn the iPad on and tap the Settings icon then Cellular Data and check this is set to On.

Step 10: Once all the set-up steps are complete, press the Start Using iPad button to begin the fun!

Wi-Fi

All iPad models can use Wi-Fi. Increasingly, hotels, cafés, restaurants, airports, railway stations and the like offer free Wi-Fi. There are also networks of public hotspots – Wi-Fi access points – where you can connect. Some are subscription based, others are free. To connect, tap the Settings icon on the Home screen. Tap Wi-Fi and then On. Under Choose a Network you'll see a list of those available. The signal strength is shown by the number of bars on the wireless symbol. The lock shows that it is a secure network and needs a password to access it. Tap the one you want to use to activate it.

Above: To activate a Wi-Fi connection choose a network from the list and enter the password.

Notifications

While it's good to know what's going on and needs your attention, previous versions of Notifications were distracting. Now you decide when – or if – notifications appear.

Access the Notification Centre

◯ Put your finger on the **bar** at the top of the screen and swipe it down. The **Notification Center** slides into view, showing what requires attention.

◯ Tap **individual items** in the **Notification Center** to switch to the app that created them.

◯ Notifications can also appear on your iPad's **Lock screen**. Slide your finger on the notification and it will **unlock the iPad** and go to the **relevant app**.

◯ You can **select** which apps send notifications and the order in which they're displayed by **tweaking your settings**:

Hot Tip

If notifications show on your Lock screen they could be seen by anyone passing by. Change this by tapping the Settings icon, then Notifications and sliding the View in Lock Screen button to Off.

1. Tap the **Settings icon** on the Home screen and select **Notifications**, then **Sort Order** and **Manual**.

2. Use the three-line handles to move the apps up and down to reflect the order you want for the notifications. When you've finished click the arrow at the top to return to **Notifications**.

Above: By tapping the Settings icon on the Home screen and selecting Notifications, you can rearrange the order in which you receive notifications and edit which apps you wish to receive them for.

Bluetooth

There are several wireless accessories that enhance your iPad – such as an external speaker or wireless headset – most of which connect via Bluetooth.

○ Tap the **Settings icon** then **General**. Tap **Bluetooth** and then switch to **On**.

○ Under **Devices** is a list of nearby **Bluetooth devices**. To connect they must be **paired** with your iPad. **Select** the device – such as a Bluetooth Wireless Keyboard – and type the numbers shown, then press **Enter** to connect.

Above: You can turn on Bluetooth within the Settings app to pair your iPad with wireless accessories such as a wireless keyboard.

Print

While the iPad saves paper, as you can carry all your documents electronically, there are times when you do need to print something out – whether it's a business report or directions to Great Aunt Maisie's house.

Above: You can print documents within some apps by tapping the arrow icon, then Print and selecting the options you want.

○ Built in to the iPad is support for printing wirelessly to **AirPrint-enabled printers**, of which there are an increasing number. All that's necessary is for the printer to be on the **same wireless network** as the iPad. You can **print direct** to AirPrint-enabled printers from built-in iPad apps such as Mail, Photos, Safari, Notes and Maps.

○ To print a document within an app, tap the arrow icon then **Print**. Press **Select Printer** and choose one from the list. Set the printer options (these are generally fairly limited and differ between apps) and tap **Print**.

○ If you don't have an AirPrint-friendly printer, all is not lost. There are **third-party apps**, such as **Printopia** (Mac only) or **Fingerprint** (Mac or Windows) that turn your computer into a print server and will let you print from your iPad or iPhone.

○ There are also apps, such as **PrintCentral** (Mac or Windows) for printing from your iPad to any wireless printer, provided it is on the **same** Wi-Fi network. They also connect to printers attached to your computer.

Search

You know the exact piece of information you need is on your iPad but can't remember where. Search will hunt through all the built-in apps, an individual app or all apps at once to

Hot Tip
The icon to the left of a Search result shows which app it is from. Simply tap the item to open.

find it. To access the Search box flick down on any page. As you start entering text, the search results begin to appear.

Above: Swipe down on any page to reveal the Search box.

NAVIGATING YOUR IPAD

The iPad is remarkably simple to use, considering the technical complexity behind it. Here's a handy primer on the gestures to use to speed your way around your iPad.

Gestures

- **Tap**: The most common gesture, the touch equivalent of the mouse click.

- **Double-tap**: Tap twice in quick succession. Primarily used for zooming in on a web page or section of text.

- **Tap and hold**: Works similarly to the right-click on a mouse. Tap on the screen and hold your finger in place and a small pop-up menu appears. In text, for example, this will give you options for cutting and pasting words or whole sentences.

- **Scroll**: The touch equivalent of using the scroll wheel on a mouse to navigate down a web page quickly. Press your finger lightly on the screen then run it up or down to move through the list or web page. On some apps, such as Contacts or Music, there is an alphabetic

Above: Apps such as Contacts and Music display an alphabetic scroll bar on the right hand side. Simply press the letter you want and you will be taken directly to the relevant part of the list.

scrollbar on the side. Press the letter you want and the page will automatically scroll to that part of the list.

- **Flick:** An extension of the scroll, this allows you to work your way through a long list, such as Contacts, more quickly. Press your finger gently on the screen then flick up or down. The faster the flick, the quicker the scroll.

- **Swipe:** Another of the primary navigational aids. Swipe left or right to move through your Home screen pages, your images in Photos or up from the bottom of the screen to view the control centre.

- **Pinch:** To zoom in or to open something put your index finger and thumb together on the screen and slowly move them apart. To zoom out do the reverse. The faster you move your fingers, the quicker the zoom.

Above: Swipe up from the bottom of the screen to access the control centre. From here, easily access your controls, including Airplane Mode and Wi-Fi. In iOS 10 there is a Night Shift button. This makes it easier to adjust the brightness of the screen at night. Swipe left and you get the Music controls.

- **Rotate:** Turn everything upside down. Just put two fingers on the screen and make a circular gesture clockwise or anti-clockwise.

Hot Tip
A two-fingered swipe has a different effect in some apps; for example, in Photos it returns you to the thumbnail view of your pictures.

Status Symbols

Just like your computer's menu bar, the iPad has a number of status icons at the top of the screen that show what's going on. Icons for your mobile and Wi-Fi connections are on the left, with other services on the right.

 Signal strength: The more bars, the stronger the network signal in your area. One bar shows little to no service, five bars and all is well.

 Carrier: At the end of the signal strength indicator is the name of the mobile data network provider, such as 3 or O2-UK.

 Wi-Fi strength: This radar-like symbol shows when you're connected to a Wi-Fi network. The more visible bars, the stronger the reception is.

 Personal hotspot: The two interlinked circles show that your iPad is sharing its high-speed mobile data connection to link a computer or other device, such as an iPod Touch, to the internet.

Hot Tip

Airplane mode turns off GPS, Bluetooth and Wi-Fi, so you won't be able to use any apps, such as Mail and Maps, which rely on these features.

 Airplane Mode: When travelling by air, this switches off any communication systems likely to interfere with the plane's controls and lets you can carry on using other apps, such as reading with iBook or writing a report with Pages. When Airplane Mode is turned on, there's a grey plane icon in the status bar.

Above: Activate Aiplane mode by toggling to On in the Settings menu. Note the plane icon in status bar.

VPN: Shows you are using a Virtual Private Network (VPN) as a secure connection across the internet to your office systems.

 Syncing icon: This rotating circle appears when the iPad is trying to make a connection over your Wi-Fi or Bluetooth network.

 Battery status: When your battery is charging, this icon shows a small lightning bolt. Beside it the percentage figures show how much battery power is left.

 Location Services: This arrow appears when an app, such as Maps, is using Location Services.

 Play button: This triangular icon appears in the status bar if you're playing a music track in iTunes.

 Bluetooth: This is turned on and is being used by your iPad to pair with another device, such as a wireless keyboard.

Above: Set an alarm by scrolling through the numbers wheel until it shows your chosen time.

 Alarm clock: Get ready for your early morning wake-up; this shows you have set an alarm in the Clock app.

 Do not Disturb: The moon icon shows that no notifications will appear on screen and that no sounds will be made while your iPad is locked or sleeping. This feature is not available on iPad 1.

Lock: The small padlock indicates that your iPad is locked.

Orientation lock: Wondering why your apps won't change from portrait to landscape? If this icon is in the status bar, it means that the orientation has been locked. To unlock it, double-press the Home button, swipe to the right and tap on the orientation button, so the lock disappears.

Multitasking

With multitasking you can switch between tasks without having to close them. You can, for example, be using one app – such as your email – and click a link that then opens another, such as Safari. Later iPads go further. Slide Over (available on iPad Pro, iPad Air or later) lets you open a second app in a sidebar. Split View (available only on the iPad Pros, iPad Air 2, and iPad mini 4) lets you have two apps open and active at the same time, while Picture in Picture (available on iPad Pro series, iPad Air or later) scales down FaceTime or the video you're watching to a corner of the display so you can open a second app.

Multitasking Screen

The Multitasking screen has all the apps currently running.

- **To open it**: Double-press on the Home button to reveal a preview page of the currently running apps.

- **To switch to another app**: Simply tap the preview of the app you want and this will open it full screen.

- **To shut down any of the open apps**: Tap and hold the app's preview page and swipe up until it disappears at the top of the screen.

- **Swipe**: If you swipe up from the bottom of the screen you have a quick way of accessing key iPad controls. There are toggle switches for Wi-Fi, Airplane Mode and

Bluetooth, quick access to the camera, calculator and torch, as well as a slider to adjust screen brightness plus a volume slider and other controls for your music.

Multitasking Gestures

A feature that's unique to the iPad and not available on other iOS devices, such as the iPhone or iPod touch, is Multitasking Gestures. Using four fingers – and your thumb if you want – you can pinch and swipe to move quickly between different apps.

◐ **Home screen pinch:** Place four or five fingers on screen in any app and bring them together to return to the Home screen.

◐ **Swipe to reveal Multitasking screen:** Open the Multitasking screen by swiping four or five fingers upwards. To close it again, swipe down.

◐ **Swipe to switch apps:** Instead of going to the Multitasking screen to move between apps, simply swipe sideways with four or five fingers and you'll go to the next open app.

Above: Swipe four or five fingers upwards to reveal the Multitasking screen which allows you to move quickly between multiple apps and pages.

Hot Tip

To turn Multitasking Gestures on, tap the Settings button on the Home screen, choose General then Multitasking and scroll down to the toggle switch to turn the feature on.

Above: To access the Multitasking function, go to the General area of the Settings app.

USING YOUR iPAD

Once you get used to the touchscreen keyboard, it's as quick and easy to use as any conventional computer keyboard. In addition, if you decide you don't want to type, ask Siri to do it for you.

On-screen Keyboard

What gives you the power to work on the iPad just as efficiently as any laptop is the virtual keyboard. In apps that use it, simply touch the area of the screen where you want to write and the keyboard appears.

The Way It Works

Unlike most keyboards, the iPad's doesn't type the letter when you press the key, but waits until you lift your finger off. There is a benefit. If you press the wrong key, simply slide your finger to the correct one before taking your finger off.

Three-in-one Keyboard

The main keyboard just has the letters and basic punctuation, with two shift keys for entering uppercase letters. To enter numbers or some of the less frequently used punctuation marks, tap the key marked .?123 to switch keyboard. To return to the first keyboard, press the ABC key, or to access the third keyboard, which has the least frequently used keys, tap #+=

Above: To display numbers and punctuation marks, press the .?123 key on the main keyboard.

Easy Punctuation

Rather than swap between keyboards, there is a faster way to add punctuation marks. Press and hold the .?123 key and slide to the punctuation you want, then lift your finger off. The punctuation mark will appear and the keyboard will revert back to letters, without you having to press the ABC key.

Cap That

Although it won't happen very often, there may be times when you need to type in all caps. To do so, double-tap the shift key. It will turn blue to show the caps lock is on. When finished, tap once more to disable caps lock. If this doesn't work, you will need to enable the caps lock. To do so, go to Settings, General then Keyboard and switch Enable Caps Lock to On.

Editing Text

No matter how good your typing is, mistakes will always happen. With the latest operating system you'll see the icons for cut, copy and paste at the top of the keyboard.

- **To correct your text**: Tap where you want the cursor to be and press the backspace key (marked with a left-pointing arrow and an X inside).

- **Magnifier**: It can be fiddly to get the cursor where you want it. You can tap-and-hold the text until a magnifier appears. Move this around the text and when you find the precise point you want, let go.

- **To select a word**: Tap the insertion point, and the selection buttons appear. Double tap a word, and it is selected and highlighted in blue with two grab points at

Hot Tip

To use both hands to type split the keyboard. Put two fingers together in the centre of the keyboard and slide them apart. Reinstate a single keyboard by putting one finger on each side of the keyboard and sliding them together.

Above: To reveal more of your screen, split the keyboard in two by placing two fingers in the centre and sliding them apart.

either end. Drag these either way to select more text. With the multi-touch cursor gesture, double-tap the keyboard with two fingers and the word where the cursor is will be selected. Triple-tap selects the whole paragraph.

○ **Once the text is selected**: option buttons appear for cutting or copying it. The Paste option will replace the highlighted text with the last text cut. Depending on the app used, other features, such as styling or text formatting, may be available.

Above: Use the magnify tool to highlight a word or selection of words with greater control and precision. Option buttons will be displayed, allowing you to copy, cut and paste as desired.

Shake It All About

A quick way to delete a message you've written or to undo an edit you've made is to shake your iPad. A dialogue box appears asking if you want to undo the last action.

Predictive Text

Rather like someone watching over your shoulder, the iPad will try to be helpful and guess what you're typing. Its suggestions will appear at the top of the QuickType keyboard. Press the relevant suggestion to accept it.

Above: To stop your iPad from predicting what you want to write toggle Predictive to off in the settings menu.

The accuracy of the iPad's suggestions should improve the more you type, as it builds up a dictionary of words you commonly use. However, some people do find this feature deeply irritating.

To stop it, go to Settings, General, Keyboard and turn off Predictive.

Voice Dictation

With the arrival of Siri on iPad 3 and later, you can dictate what you want to write, rather than use the on-screen keyboard to type your text.

1. Check that voice dictation is turned on. Press the Settings icon, select General, followed by Siri.

2. You will need to be connected to the internet, either through a Wi-Fi connection or over the mobile network, as dictation is controlled by Siri. This is the voice-commanded personal assistant on your iPad. Everything you say to Siri is sent over the internet to Apple's servers to be interpreted, and the answer or response is then sent back to the iPad.

3. Open the app you want to use, such as Pages for a document or Mail for email.

Step 1: Turning on Siri in the General area of the Settings menu allows you to dictate what you want to write.

Hot Tip

The more you use dictation, the better it gets as it adapts to your accent.

Step 4: Touch the microphone icon at the bottom of the on-screen keyboard to begin dictating your text to Siri.

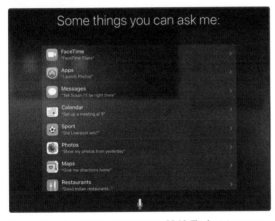

Step 7: You can make corrections using the on-screen keyboard.

Some things you can ask me:

FaceTime
"FaceTime Claire"

Apps
"Launch Photos"

Messages
"Tell Susan I'll be right there"

Calendar
"Set up a meeting at 9"

Sport
"Did Liverpool win?"

Photos
"Show my photos from yesterday"

Maps
"Give me directions home"

Restaurants
"Good Indian restaurants…"

Above: Siri works with many more apps in iOS 10. This list is just some of the options you have to use Apple's voice-activated digital assistant.

Hot Tip

Any app that uses the on-screen keyboard should allow dictation, as the feature is built into the iPad OS, not the program.

4. Tap the screen, so the on-screen keyboard appears. In the lower left-hand corner is the voice dictation logo, which looks like an old-fashioned radio microphone.

5. Tap this and start speaking. You will need to include punctuation commands, such as comma, new paragraph, etc. Take care to pronounce special symbols, such as the 'at sign' – @ – seen in emails, clearly.

6. When you've finished dictating, tap the microphone icon again. Your text will appear soon.

7. If you make a mistake, or the dictated text is wrongly transcribed, simply tap where you want to edit and the on-screen keyboard appears. Use this to make your corrections. Siri's done well here – only the end of 'fashioned' has been left off.

8. To add more, repeat the steps.

APPS

Your iPad comes with just 25 or so apps already loaded, covering the basics from writing notes to playing music. When you want to do more, such as tracking the stars or mind mapping, you can be sure there is an app for it.

GET AND USE APPS

There's no shortage of apps for your iPad. Currently, there are more than 750,000 free or paid-for apps in the App Store that are specifically designed for the iPad.

Finding New Apps

You get new apps through Apple's App Store, which is accessed through iTunes on your computer or the App Store app, preloaded on the iPad.

Above: When the App Store is open, five useful buttons are displayed on the lower toolbar.

Apple ID

To use the App Store, you have to be connected to the internet (via Wi-Fi or mobile) and have an Apple ID. You probably entered this when you activated your iPad. If not, go to Settings, iTunes & App Stores (Store on iPad 1) and enter your details or create a new ID.

Using the App Store App

Accessing the App Store from the iPad itself lets you download new apps directly. Tap the App Store icon to open it and you'll see there are five buttons on the lower toolbar.

○ **Featured**: Good for browsing, this screen shows new and noteworthy apps, what's hot and so on. Along the top you can select apps from specific interests, such as games or education.

○ **Top Charts**: Shows the most popular paid-for and free apps, as well as the top-grossing apps in the store. Scroll down to see more.

○ **Explore**: Apple will recommend new apps for you based on your location or you can search for specific categories that interest you.

In the purchased section, tap Not On This iPad and you'll see all the apps you have bought that have not yet been downloaded to your iPad.

○ **Purchased**: This lists all the apps (both paid-for and free) you have downloaded to any device, such as your computer, using the same Apple ID. If you've deleted an app you want to restore, find it in the list and tap the Cloud icon to download it. You won't have to pay again.

○ **Updates**: The badge shows how many updates are available for the apps on your iPad. Click the Update or Update All button to download and install them.

iTunes

Open iTunes on your computer and click iTunes Store on the top bar, then Apps from the top menu. Click the iPad button at the top of the screen to select that section of the store.

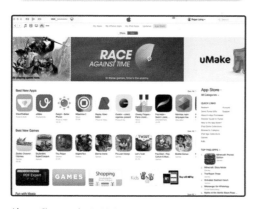

Above: Choosing the iPad link in iTunes on your computer allows you to dowload apps and then sync them to your iPad.

Choosing Your Apps

There are specially selected lists of new and popular apps. Often these are related to seasonal or topical events, ranging from winter holidays to Halloween and major sporting occasions. To find out more about an app, click its icon to access a dedicated page with details of what it does, screenshots, and customer ratings and reviews for each version. On the iPad this opens in a pop up window when you tap the icon.

Step 1: Clicking the i in the bottom-right corner of an app icon opens a pop-up iinformation window.

Downloading Apps from the iPad

1. Once you've found the app you would like to get, downloading it is very quick and easy. Tap an app's icon in the app store to open a pop-up information window.

2. Scroll down to read a description or use the tabs to see ratings and reviews by other customers or related apps from the same developer that you might be interested in.

3. Tap the price button and then tap Buy. If it's not a paid-for app, tap the Get button (previously labelled Free) then Install.

Hot Tip

Tap an app to pause download (useful if there are other apps you want to get first).
Tap again to resart.

Step 2: The pop-up information window allows you to read ratings and reviews before you decide to download an app.

Step 4: Once you have decided to download an app, tap the Buy or Get button and then Install.

Above: A blue circle beside an app shows it has been updated to a newer version in the background but not yet opened.

Downloading Apps from iTunes

Buying an app in iTunes is the same as on the iPad. Select the app and click the price button. This time, though, it is downloaded to your computer. The app is installed on your iPad when you next sync (provided the computer and iPad are both linked to the

4. To stop you buying the same app twice (which did previously happen), the button now says Open, Install or Update.

5. You may be asked to enter your Apple ID and password. Tap OK when ready.

6. The button is replaced by a circular blue progress bar. You can move off the page and open other apps while this is happening. Once the download is complete, the app appears on your Home screen and is ready to open.

7. If the app download is interrupted for any reason, it will start again automatically the next time you connect to the internet.

Hot Tip

Sync all your apps to your iPad automatically, no matter where they were originally downloaded. Tap the Settings icon then iTunes & App Stores (Store on iPad 1) and go to the Automatic Downloads section. Slide the switch beside Apps to On.

same Apple ID). Similarly, any apps downloaded to the iPad directly will also be automatically added to iTunes. To automatically update apps when a new version is available go to iTunes & App Store and switch on the button beside Updates.

Open and Close Apps

Simply tap the app's icon to open it. To close it and return to the Home screen, just press the Home button. In fact, the app is just suspended. To fully close it, double-press the Home button to open the Multitasking screen, tap and hold the app's preview page and swipe up.

Arranging Your Apps

With so many apps available, you may soon have several pages of apps. You can rearrange them in two ways – on the iPad and in iTunes.

- **On the iPad**: Tap and hold the icon until it starts jiggling, then drag and drop it where you want it. If you want to move it to the next page of apps, drag it to the edge of the screen. When finished, press the Home button to stop the icons jiggling.

Above: Arrange apps on the Home screen of your iPad by tapping and holding an icon until it starts jiggling, and then dragging and dropping to rearrange

- **In iTunes**: Connect your iPad to iTunes, select your iPad from the top bar and then Apps from the menu. Click and drag the icons where you want them.

Organizing Apps in Folders

Several related apps can be grouped in folders. Tap and hold the icon of one app and drag it on top of another you wish to group it with. When you lift your finger, a folder will open with both apps inside. The folder is automatically given a name based on the apps included. To change this tap in the box to access the on-screen keyboard. Press the Home button when finished.

To ungroup the apps, tap the folder to open, then tap and hold one of the app's icons until it starts jiggling. Once in Edit mode, drag and drop each app icon out of the folder.

Above: Ungroup apps by tapping open a folder, holding an app icon until it jiggles and then dragging apps out the folder.

Remove Apps

To delete an app, tap and hold its icon, then press the small X in a white circle that appears in the top-left corner. Be sure you want to do this, as any data entered – such as financial information in an accounts app – will also be permanently removed.

Running iPhone Apps

Some iPhone apps can work just as well on the iPad. Because they are not specifically designed for the iPad they will usually run in a small window in the middle. You can enlarge the app by tapping the 2x button in the lower-right. If it's blurry or blocky, restore it to its original size by tapping the 1x button.

Changing App Settings

Most apps keep the options for changing the way they work inside the app itself. Confusingly, though, some apps have a second set of options inside the iPad's Settings app. To access these, tap the Settings icon and select the app from the list on the left. The available options are shown on the right.

Hot Tip

If you tap and hold an app and the small black X doesn't appear, it means it is one of the default apps, pre-loaded on the iPad. These can't be deleted.

SYNCING

It's easier than ever to keep your personal information, music, video files and apps on your iPad in sync using iTunes, iCloud or other online cloud services.

SYNCING WITH ITUNES

As well as keeping all your information up-to-date, syncing is a good safety measure. Each time you sync your iPad with iTunes, a backup is made of all your information. If you lose your iPad or it needs to be reset, you can restore all your data from these backups. It is also the quickest way to transfer large files, such as photos, music or videos.

Syncing by USB: Step-by-step

1. Connect your iPad to the computer by USB cable. Open iTunes on your computer and your iPad is listed in the top bar.

Step 1: To sync your iPad with your computer connect via USB cable. You can then click the Info tab and select options to sync contacts and calendars.

2. Click the Summary tab and you'll see various information about your iPad, along with several options. These include checking for software updates, choosing where you want to back up your data and other general settings, such as automatically opening iTunes when the iPad is connected.

3. Select the Info tab for options to sync your contacts and calendars with related Apple apps on the iPad. If you are using iTunes on a PC the available options are more limited.

4. Select the Music tab and check Sync Music. As the iPad has a smaller capacity than your computer, you probably don't want to sync your entire music library. Instead check Selected playlists, artists, albums and genres. Then go through the different categories and check the box beside the ones you want to transfer.

5. Go through the other tabs – Apps, Tones, Movies, TV Shows, Podcasts, Books and Photos – and select what you want to sync. If some of the tabs mentioned aren't visible, don't worry: it just means you have none of that type of content in your iTunes library. When finished, click Apply to start the sync.

Syncing Wirelessly

Instead of connecting by USB cable to sync, you can use Wi-Fi. Ironically, though, to do so, you first have to connect your iPad with iTunes using a USB cable.

1. Your iPad will show in the top bar in iTunes. Click this and scroll to Options on the Summary tab.

2. Check the box next to Sync with this iPad over Wi-Fi and click Apply in the bottom-right corner.

3. To sync wirelessly, your iPad has to be connected to a power source and be on the same Wi-Fi network as the computer. The computer must also have iTunes open. If you still don't see your iPad in the list of devices, quit and restart iTunes or restart your iPad.

4. Configure your sync options just as you would with the USB connection.

Hot Tip

If you check **Manually Manage Music and Videos**, automatic syncing is turned off. To move songs and movies, first go to the View menu in iTunes and select **Show Sidebar**. Then drag and drop tracks or clips from your iTunes library onto the iPad icon.

Above: Set up wireless sync using iTunes, so that you can sync your devices over Wi-Fi.

iCLOUD

Apple's online service enables you to keep everything in sync and store your music, photos, documents and apps securely.

Step-by-step

1. To set up and configure iCloud: tap Settings then select iCloud. Sign in with your Apple ID and password, or create one if you haven't yet done so.

2. Choose which iCloud services you want to use: slide the switch to On.

3. iCloud Drive lets you safely store PDFs, images and any other kind of document in iCloud and sync it with your iPad using the iCloud Drive app.

4. Photos: when you take a photo with any iOS device you have, it will be shared and show up in the Photos app on your iPad.

5. Mail, Contacts, Calendars, Reminders, Notes and News: these sync with relevant apps.

6. Safari: this syncs your bookmarks, any open tabs and reading list.

7. Backup: sends your data wirelessly to iCloud.

8. Keychain: keeps your passwords and credit card information safe and accessible.

9. Find My iPad: help to locate your lost or stolen iPad.

Step 2: To choose which iCloud services you want to use, toggle switches to On or Off accordingly.

ALTERNATIVE CLOUD SERVICES

While iCloud works well with the Mac and iOS devices (iPad, iPhone and iPod touch), not all its features are available to those who don't use Apple software. Fortunately, there are many cloud services that work just as well with the iPad.

In the Cloud

Cloud services are online storage and syncing facilities. Your content is uploaded – copied – to the company's data centre. Although this is described metaphorically as being 'in the cloud' it is actually in a very down-to-earth city location.

Your stored content can be accessed via the internet, through any browser, or downloaded wirelessly to your computer or iPad, whenever and wherever you want.

Cloud Apps

Many cloud services have an app for the iPad. Using this, you can access your documents and files stored in the cloud and keep them in sync. Several also have desktop software for your Mac or PC that works in a similar way.

Cloud services you can use direct from your iPad include Google Drive, OneDrive from Microsoft, Dropbox and Evernote.

Like iCloud, most cloud services offer a free account with a fairly generous amount of storage – typically around 5GB – and paid-for upgrades if more is needed.

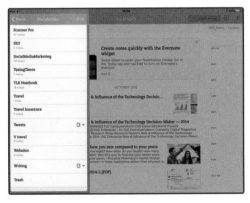

Above: Evernote for iPad is an example of a cloud service which has an app that you can use to access documents in the cloud.

GETTING CONECTED

SURFING THE NET

Through the built-in Safari browser and your Wi-Fi or mobile connection to the internet, you can surf the web, view your favourite sites, update your blog and download files.

ACCESS WEBSITES

The high-quality screen makes browsing clear and bright, and with the Retina display on the latest iPads the web has never looked so good.

Browsing

- **Safari** on the iPad is a little different from the one on your **Mac** or **PC**. To open it, **tap** the Safari icon in the dock of commonly used applications at the bottom of the screen.

- When you open Safari, it will show the **last web page** you viewed, if any, or a favourite page you select.

- In the **top bar**, tap the screen and type the web address – **URL** – you want to visit, using the on-screen keyboard. As you type, you'll see suggestions of previous pages you've visited, which you can **select** by tapping the address in the list. Tap **Go** when you've finished.

> ## Hot Tip
> Made a mistake? Clear the address bar at any time by tapping the X button on the far right.

Above: To visit a website use the onscreen keyboard to type the web address and press go.

Tab That

Just like your desktop browser, you can have several web pages open at once, in separate tabbed windows. To open a new window, tap the + button at the end of the tab bar and enter the web address. Switch between the windows by tapping the tab you want. To close just that page, tap the X button in the left corner.

Cloud Button

If you've been surfing the web using Safari on your Mac, you can carry on from the same place on your iPad by tapping the View open tabs icon (two squares on top of each other) in the Safari toolbar. This will show you the tabs that are currently open on your other iOS devices and Mac, provided they are also set up to use iCloud.

FASTER BROWSING

The iPad 3 and all later iPad models support the somewhat new 4G technology, which enables much faster browsing and quicker download speeds for videos and such like.

4G LTE

The latest iPads with mobile connections support the next generation of mobile broadband – 4G LTE (Long Term Evolution). In fact, it's so 'next generation' that these 4G fourth generation networks aren't universally available yet and are still being rolled out in different countries. The advantage of 4G is that it

Above: Tap the View open tabs icon to access sites which are currently open on your Mac or other iOS devices which have iCloud activated.

is about five times faster than 3G and more reliable. Not only are browsing and downloading faster, but there's also less choppiness when you stream a video or watch TV – that is, fewer stops as the iPad struggles to keep up. Even without 4G, the new iPads support the latest and fastest versions of 3G. With their powerful new antennae inside they are less likely to lose the connection.

NAVIGATING THE WEB

Just like your computer browser, Safari lets you move backwards and forwards between open web pages using the left and right pointers on the top bar. However, there are other novel ways to navigate individual pages.

Viewing Web Pages

- **Scroll the page:** Drag your finger up and down the screen. The scrollbar on the right shows where you are. For faster scrolling, flick your finger up or down the page.

- **Unpinch:** This lets you zoom in on part of the page. Put two fingers together on the screen where you want to enlarge the page and move them apart. Put two fingers either side of the screen and move them together (pinch) to reverse this.

- **Zoom in to images** and text by double-tapping the screen. Zoom out by repeating the double-tap.

- **Once zoomed in**, tap the screen and drag the page left or right. A horizontal scrollbar at the bottom of the screen shows where you are on the page.

Uncluttered Websites

Some web pages are so full of text and ads that they can be very difficult to read. Safari Reader solves this by presenting a stripped down version of the page. Tap the Reader button, to the left of the address field, and ads are removed, leaving just text and pictures.

Private Browsing

If you don't want to leave a trail of the websites you've visited – such as the

Above: You can navigate web pages by pinching and unpinching to zoom in and out, and dragging up and down to scroll.

jewellery store where you have been looking for presents – turn on private browsing.

1. Tap the View open tabs icon (two squares) then tap Private and the + sign to open a new browser window. Now sites you visit won't appear in iCloud tabs or be added to the History on your iPad. You also lose the convenience of Safari saving any website login details.

2. With Safari in private mode the top and bottom bars are black rather than the usual grey.

3. For further privacy you can also clear your history (the list of sites you have visited), as well as cookies and other website data.

Hot Tip
The Reader button doesn't appear with every web page you view. It has to be supported by the website you're visiting, which many commercial sites won't do, as they want their ads to show.

Watching Flash Videos

When browsing the web with Safari, you may find that videos on the page won't play, as they need Adobe Flash to run, which isn't supported on the iPad. Some sites, such as YouTube, get round this by automatically changing the video format in the background. If not, there are alternative browsers for the iPad that can play Flash, such as Skyfire, available from the App Store.

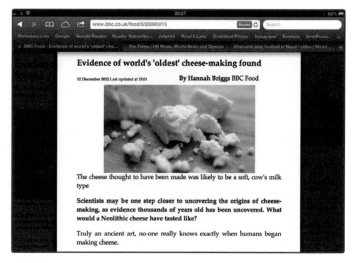

Above: Select the Safari Reader button to display an uncluttered version of the webpage which has ads removed, leaving only text and pictures.

SEARCH

Search the web, using your preferred search engine, direct from the iPad.

1. **The Search box**: This is now part of Safari's address bar. Simply tap the bar and use the pop-up keyboard to enter what you are searching for.

2. **As you type**: A list of suggestions will appear as you type. If none are correct, finish entering your text and tap the Go button on the keyboard.

3. **Search term**: You can also look for your search term on the web page you're currently viewing. Scroll to the end of the list of suggestions and tap On This Page.

4. **Google**: This the default search engine used by Safari. To change this, tap Settings, Safari, then Search Engine and select the one you'd prefer.

SAVE THE WEB

As you browse the web, Safari offers several ways to share the pages you like or save them for reading later.

Sharing

Tap the Share button on the top bar for various ways to spread the word about a web page. Mail the link, text it or post it to your status on Facebook and Twitter. For easy

Above: Press the Home button to search the web by dictating your request to Siri.

access, add it to your Home Screen or Reading List, save it as a PDF to iBooks or some other cloud service and bookmark, or print it, if an AirPrint printer is available.

Reading List

If you don't have time to read something that interests you, view it later. Tap the Share button, then touch Add to Reading List. The page isn't stored on your iPad but is synced with iCloud, so you can access the page, using any of your iOS devices, via the internet.

Instead of repeatedly filling in your personal contact details on web forms, use AutoFill. Enable it by tapping Settings, Safari and selecting AutoFill preferences.

To view your Reading List, tap Bookmarks and then the spectacle icons for Add to Reading list. Once you have visited the page, it no longer shows in the Unread list but can still be accessed by selecting Show All.

BOOKMARKS

To add a page to your bookmarks, tap the Share button, then Bookmark. To access your bookmarks, tap the open book icon on the top bar. Using iCloud, you can synchronize your bookmarks between your iPad, computer and other iOS devices.

To change your bookmarks, tap Edit in the top corner. Press the red '–' sign to delete one. To reorder your bookmarks, tap and hold the three-line grab handles and move them up or down the list. When finished, tap Done.

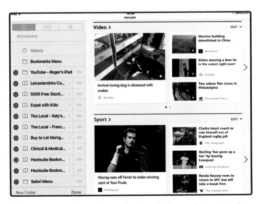

Left View, visit and reorder your bookmarked pages by tapping the open book icon in the top bar.

MESSAGING

Need to send a message to a friend? Using the built-in Messages app, you can text anyone who has an iPhone, iPod Touch or iPad for free – and even send pictures or video.

Step 1: Check iMessage is turned on by selecting the Messages option within Settings.

Step 4: Tap the New Message icon, start typing in the To box to bring up other iMessage users.

TEXTING

The beauty of iMessage, the name that Apple has given to its messaging system, is that since iOS 5 it is built in.

How to Text: Step-by-step

1. Go to Settings, Messages and make sure that iMessage is turned on.

2. Launch the Messages app. If it's not already entered, you'll have to give your Apple ID and password to activate the service. Then simply tap Sign In.

3. Enter the email address you want to use to send messages from. It can be any email address that you own; it doesn't have to be the same one used with your Apple ID. Tap Next.

4. Open Messages and tap the new message icon (pen and paper) at the top of the screen. Start writing in the To: line and a pop-up box listing your relevant contacts will appear.

5. Tap the name of the selected iMessage user, type your message and press the blue Send button.

6. In true messaging style, your conversation is shown as a series of speech bubbles: your message on the right, your friend's reply on the left. When someone is replying to you, there's a bubble with three dots in the chat window.

Step 6: Sent and received messages are shown in speech bubbles.

Group Messaging

You can send messages to a group. Just write their names in the To: line or select them from your Contacts.

Go Multimedia

To add a picture tap the Camera icon beside the text box. In the pop-up box, choose to send an existing image from your photo library or select Take Photo or Video and add a new picture or video clip.

Above: In iOS 10 the text box in Messages has three buttons beside it for adding photos, from the camera or photo library, sketches and other apps.

Contact Details

In a conversation, tap Details, then tap the Information icon and you can see the contact details of the person.

Cleaning Up

To forward your message tap and hold, then press More, select any additional items and then tap the Forward arrow. Follow a similar process and choose the Dustbin icon to delete messages. To remove the whole conversation, select it from the left-hand menu and swipe your finger right to left and tap the Delete button.

EMAIL

If you can't bear to be parted from your email, the Mail app lets you connect to your online mailbox and will even notify you when you've got mail.

SETTING UP ACCOUNTS

To access your email, you first need to set up details of your email service. Although you can now use iCloud to sync your Apple Mail with the iPad, it is best to set up other email accounts directly on your iPad.

Syncing Your Email via iCloud

1. Using the Mail app you can sync your Apple email addresses with the iPad using iCloud.

2. Go to Settings, then iCloud.

3. Make sure the toggle button beside Mail is on and showing green. Now all your emails to your iCloud address are synced with the iPad.

Add Email Accounts Direct to Your iPad

You access your emails through the Mail app, but you set up the account using the Settings app.

1. Tap Settings, then Mail, Contacts, Calendars and Add Account.

2. You will see the most popular web-based mail services listed, including Gmail, Outlook.com, AOL etc. There's also Microsoft Exchange, which is used by many schools and companies.

3. Tap the button for your email service if it's listed and enter your name, email address, password and a description, then tap Save.

4. If it's not listed, select Other and enter your account details manually – you can get them from your Internet Service Provider.

CONFIGURING MAIL

There are several ways to customize Mail to make it work in a way that suits you so that you can keep up-to-date with your emails without being overwhelmed.

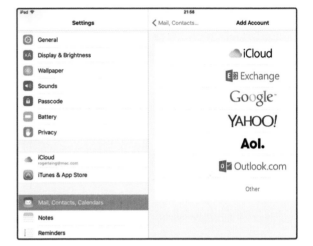

Step 2: Choose your email provider from the list, or tap Other to add your account details.

Preferences

Select how you want to organize your emails in Settings, Mail, Contacts, Calendars, then scroll to Mail.

- **Show**: This selects how many messages, from 50 to 1,000, to display in your inbox.

- **Preview**: Change how many lines of text from each email are shown in List view.

- **Show To/Cc Label**: This shows if you are the main recipient of an email or if it was copied to you.

- **Swipe Options**: Lets you set what actions – such as Mark as Read – are taken when you swipe left or right.

- **Flag Style**: Change whether you want this as a colour or shape.

- **Ask Before Deleting**: This is a useful precaution if you often delete emails accidentally.

○ **Load Remote Images**: Turn this off to save bandwidth, if you often download your email over a mobile connection.

○ **Organize By Thread**: Turn this on and all replies to an email will be grouped under the original message.

Other options let you send a blind copy of every outgoing email to yourself; indent text quoted in a reply; and set the default email account to be used by iPad apps.

Above: Choose how your emails are organized by toggling options On or Off in the Mail settings list.

Configuring How Email Is Received

Where it's supported, you can have new emails pushed to you automatically or fetched from the server at a set interval you determine.

1. Tap Settings, then Mail, Contacts, Calendars and select Fetch New Data.

Above: Choose whether to receive your emails by Push or Fetch, and how frequently this will happen.

2. If you have an email service where the server will automatically 'push' any new emails received to you, such as iCloud or Microsoft Exchange, then select Push.

3. If not, select Fetch. Then choose how frequently you want Mail to check for new emails, ranging from Every 15 Minutes to Hourly. The more frequently it checks, the greater the drain on your battery.

4. Select each account and then choose which schedule you would like to apply. Selecting Manual effectively turns off automatic email checking.

> ## Hot Tip
> **Signature adds your personal sign off to every email you send. Go to Settings, Mail, Contacts, Calendars, then choose Signature and enter your text. This is also where you delete the annoying default signature added by Apple: *Sent from my iPad*.**

WORKING WITH EMAIL

Use the built-in Mail app to send and receive your emails when you are connected to the internet.

Using Mail

Mail shows all your inboxes – the mailboxes for incoming emails – in one list with the Accounts underneath.

- At the top of the list is **All Inboxes**. This is a **single inbox** for all the emails you receive from any account. Alternatively, you can select the inbox for an **individual account**, such as your main personal or work account.

- The list appears **automatically** when the iPad is in **landscape view**. In **portrait view** flick your finger from the **left** of the screen to show the list; flick from the **right** side of the screen to close it again.

Receive Mail

1. When you tap the inbox, there's a list of all your emails. Each one shows the sender's name, when it was sent, the subject line and a preview of the first few lines of the message.

2. Drag the list down to check for new messages. Tap the message preview, and the full message opens in the main window.

3. If you tap the sender's name, you have the option to add them as a new contact or add the email address to an existing contact. You can also add them to your VIP list.

4. A message at the top shows how many items are grouped together into a thread, because they all have the same subject line.

5. Flick to scroll through the message or messages if it's a thread. Double-tap or pinch to zoom in on the text or images. Touch and hold an image for options to save, copy or share it.

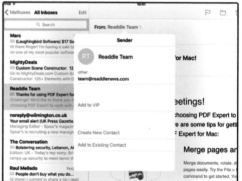

6. If there's a word in the message you're not familiar with, look it up. Double-tap to select the word, using the grab handles if necessary, and then tap Define in the pop-up menu bar.

7. To zip back to the start of the email, tap the iPad status bar at the top of the screen.

Above: Tapping the name of an email sender gives you the option to add the address to your contact or VIP lists.

Organize Your Messages

Along Mail's top bar are several icons that help you organize your messages.

○ **Flag**: Tap this and select Flag to show the message is important (it will appear with an Orange flag beside it in the list)

Hot Tip

Tap and hold the Home button and ask Siri to 'check my email', and a list of the latest emails appears. Tap the one you want, and it opens in the main Mail window (on iPad 3 and later).

or Mark as Unread (which is shown by a small blue circle), or Move to Junk.

○ **Folder**: Tap, and the list box shows the folders (mailboxes) for that account. Select a folder, and the message is moved there.

○ **Bin**: This deletes the message.

○ **Arrow**: Tap this for options to Reply, Forward or Print your message.

○ **Edit**: Use this to apply an action to several messages at once. Tap the Edit button at the top of the Inboxes List, then touch the messages you want. Press the Delete, Move or Mark (as Unread) buttons as required.

Above: Tap the flag icon in Mail's top bar to Flag an important message or Mark as Unread.

Search

This is handy if you want to find that elusive email or group together several on the same topic or from the same person. Tap in the Search box at the top of the screen and enter your phrase. As you type Mail suggests ways you can refine your search, such as

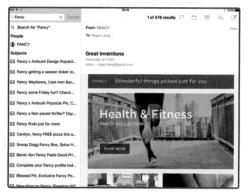

Above: To find particular emails stored in your mail box, type a phrase in the search box and select the relevant option to choose where to search.

limiting it to certain People, Subjects, Dates or Mailboxes. From the results, click the Edit button and select the emails you want to delete/archive, move or mark, as appropriate.

Delete Messages

To delete a message, flick its title in the message list. If the email is open, you can also use the delete button in the top bar. To delete several emails at once, click the Edit button, select the messages and click the red delete button.

Deleting the Archive

Given the huge amounts of space some services offer for email storage, some email providers, such as Gmail, don't delete messages but archive them.

1. Flick across a message in the list and the normal Delete button is shown as Archive. Tap this and the message is removed from that inbox but still remains in the All Mail folder.

2. To delete the message, tap Settings, then Mail, Contacts, Calendars. Tap the relevant account, then the account name, select Advanced and under Move Discarded Messages Into: select Deleted Mailbox.

Hot Tip

If you forward an email, you can include attachments from the original, which you can't if you just Reply to a message.

Send Email: Step-by-step

1. To write a new email, tap the Paper and Pen icon at the top of Mail or if you're replying or forwarding a message, select the curved arrow at the top.

2. In the New Message box that opens, add the recipient's email address. You can type this in or tap the + sign to select them from your Contacts list.

3. If you choose the wrong name, simply tap it and press the backspace key on the keyboard to delete it.

4. Add anyone you're copying the message to. Use Bcc – blind copying – if you're sending it to lots of people, such as a mailing list, and you don't want to show all their addresses.

5. Tap From and choose the account you are using to send it. Then you can write your email.

Above: Forward a message by clicking on the curved arrow at the top of an email and select the Forward option.

6. To format the text, tap and use the grab handles to select all the text you want to include. Tap BIU and then choose Bold, Italic or Underline.

7. To add an attachment, tap where you want to add it and select the Camera icon on the keyboard to insert a Photo or Video or the paper clip to attach a document. Select the source, then the item and tap the Use button.

Hot Tip
You can resize photo attachments, which is particularly useful when sending your email over a mobile connection. Once the photo is attached, tap Images, then Image size in the header section and choose Small, Medium or Large, as appropriate.

8. When you're happy with your message, press the Send button in the top-right corner. If you're not yet ready to send, tap the Cancel button and choose the Save Draft option.

VIP MAIL

Messages from people you choose as important to you – your close family, best friends, boss, etc. – appear in their own VIP mailbox. They will also have a VIP star icon beside their name in the message preview.

Adding VIPs

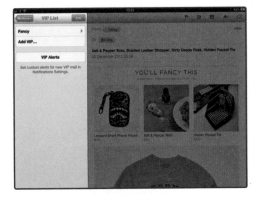

- **To add a sender to your VIP list**: Tap their name in the From field in an email and select Add to VIP from the pop-up box.

- **To manage your VIP list**: Touch the white arrow in a blue circle icon. Here you can add more people and set up alerts for the arrival of VIP mail.

Above: Tap the VIP mailbox to add and remove contacts to your VIP list and set up alerts.

VIDEO CALLING

If you have an iPad 2 or later, you can use the built-in cameras to have great video chats with other Apple users via FaceTime or use Skype to reach more of your contacts.

Above: Activate FaceTime by selecting the FaceTime option in your settings list and toggling to On.

FACETIME

With the iPad's FaceTime app you can make free video calls over the internet from anywhere in the world.

Setting up Your Video Calls

As well as a camera-equipped iPad, you'll need to be connected to the internet to use FaceTime. The person you are calling must also have an iPad, iPhone or iPod Touch with forward-facing camera or a Mac computer with camera and FaceTime.

1. Before you start, activate FaceTime by going to Settings, then FaceTime.

2. FaceTime identifies you through your Apple ID, the email address and password you use for accessing the App Store. You can either use your existing ID or create a new one.

3. Next, select which of your email addresses to use as your contact point with your FaceTime account.

4. Turn on Calls from iPhone and you can use your iPhone's mobile connection to make and receive calls when it's near your iPhone and on Wi-Fi.

FaceTime Calls: Step-by-Step

1. To make a FaceTime call, tap the FaceTime app to open it. A list of previous calls is on the left. Enter the name, email address or number of the person you want to call in the search box or tap the + icon to view your contacts.

2. To make a call, tap the name of the person, then the camera icon for a video FaceTime or the phone for just audio.

3. When they answer, there will be a pause while the video chat is set up. Once connected, your face will shrink to a small thumbnail, while the person you are calling is pictured in the main window.

4. During the call, drag your picture to a different position if it's in the way.

5. Tap the microphone icon on the menu to temporarily mute sound (the picture won't be affected). Tap again to restore it.

6. Tap the camera icon to switch from the front camera, showing you, to the back camera, which will show what's around you.

7. To finish the chat, tap the telephone icon marked End.

Step 3: Video images of yourself and your contact appear once the call is set up.

Step 5: Tap the microphone icon to mute sound, and tap again to unmute.

Step 6: Tap the camera icon to change between using your front and back iPad cameras.

Hot Tip

You can switch apps during a chat, if, for example, you want to look something up. Press the Home button, then the icon for the app you want. You can still chat but there will be no picture. Tap the green bar at the top of the screen to resume the video call.

SKYPE

Unlike FaceTime, Skype offers free video and voice chat that lets you stay in touch with friends and family no matter what computer or mobile device they use. Owned by Microsoft, it also replaces their highly popular instant messaging program, Windows Live Messenger.

Using Skype: Step-by-Step

Before using Skype, you have to set up an account. Open your Safari web browser on the iPad and type in the address www.skype.com.

1. On the Home page tap the blue Join Skype button and fill in the form, which includes creating your Skype username and password. Alternatively, you can sign up using a Microsoft account, such as Messenger or Hotmail, an email programme like Outlook or your Facebook account.

2. If you haven't already, download the Skype for iPad app from iTunes. Open the app and enter your Skype sign in details.

3. Skype asks permission to add your contacts. Alternatively, you can tap the contacts icon with a + button and enter a name or email address in the Search box to find someone.

Step 3: Tap the contacts icon with a + button to use Skype Search for people you want to add to your contact list.

4. Once you have discovered them, select them and in the screen that opens tap Add Contact. Enter a message asking them to accept you as a contact and tap send.

5. Once you have built up your Contacts list, simply tap the contact you want to call. Choose the type of call you want to make – it can be a Video Call, Voice Call or Chat (Instant Messaging conversation).

6. The controls are much the same as for FaceTime, with the menu bar at the bottom and the main window displaying the video with your picture inset.

7. To send a text message during your video chat, tap the message icon – a speech bubble – and type it in the pop-up box that appears. Tap the message button again to close the window.

8. End the call by tapping the phone receiver icon.

9. By default, Skype will show you as online when you login. You can change this status by selecting the My Info icon. Click on Status and you have the option to say you're Away, Do not disturb or Offline. If you set it to Invisible you'll appear to be offline to all your contacts but you can still use Skype as usual.

Phone Home, Cheaply

As Skype-to-Skype voice calls are free, they are a very popular way for people to stay in touch, wherever they are in the world, without running up huge phone bills. Low-cost calls can also be made to ordinary landline phones and mobiles by signing up to Skype's unlimited plan or buying pay-as-you-go credit.

Hot Tip

You can chat with anyone, anywhere using the Skype app with a Wi-Fi or 3G connection on any iPad. But while you can send and receive video using the front or back camera with the iPad 2 or above, you can only receive video on the first generation iPad.

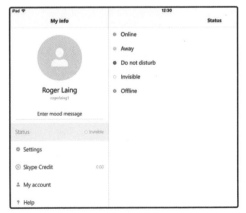

Above: If you do not want to always appear 'Online' but still use Skype, change your status to invisible.

SOCIAL MEDIA

The popularity of social media is such that Apple has built support for Facebook and Twitter in to the iPad operating system itself. Now you can Tweet, update your status, post a photo, your location or a link direct from several of the built-in apps.

FACEBOOK

As one of the most popular sites on the web, with more than one billion users, it's natural that Facebook is now directly accessible from your iPad.

Setting up Facebook

Support for Facebook is built in to all but the first generation iPad. With it you can do all you normally can, from browsing your newsfeed to adding photos, without opening the Facebook app.

1. To set up Facebook, tap Settings and then Facebook. If you haven't already installed the app, do so by clicking the Install button.

2. Enter your Facebook Username and Password and tap Sign In. The pop-up window explains what you allow by signing into Facebook from the iPad's operating system. In essence, this is agreeing to:

   ○ **Merge** your Facebook friends' details with your Contacts, so that if they update their details, their entry in your Contacts is also immediately updated.

Above: Set up Facebook through your Settings for an integrated social networking experience.

- **Download** your Facebook events to your calendar.

- **Allow** you to post photos, update your status, and send messages and other content to Facebook.

- **Enable** other apps on your iPad to access your Facebook account. To do so, they first have to ask your permission and make clear what information they will use and how. You can withdraw your permission at any time.

3. If you don't accept this, tap the Cancel button; otherwise touch Sign In.

4. Ironically, having just allowed Facebook to access your Contacts and Calendar, you can now refuse either one or both, by turning off the button beside the relevant icon in the Allow These Apps to Use Your Account section.

5. If you tap Update All Contacts, your information will be shared with Facebook, so they can update photos and usernames.

Hot Tip

On the original iPad you can upgrade the operating system to iOS 5, which includes Twitter integration but not Facebook integration, which was only introduced later. The only way to access Facebook on iPad 1 is to download the standalone app from iTunes.

Above: Choose whether you want Facebook to have access to your Contacts and Calendar by toggling the buttons to On or Off.

Using Facebook on the iPad

- **Update your status**: Tap the Facebook icon to open the app. At the top of your iPad, above your News Feed is the Status Update box. Write your message, then tap the Post button.

○ **Share URLs:** When you're browsing the internet with Safari and come across a link you'd like to post on Facebook, tap the Share button, then Facebook.

○ **Send pictures:** To send photos direct from your photo library, select the image you want to post in Photos, tap the Share button and then Facebook. In the Update box you'll see the image. Tap the Album icon to choose the photo album on Facebook to which it will be posted. In Camera, tap the roll of images, then press the Share button and Facebook as above.

○ **Share your current location:** In the Maps app, tap the pin that marks where you are, then the Share button and select Facebook.

○ **Like apps, music and more:** The Facebook Like button is now in iTunes and the App Store, so you can show your friends what you appreciate without leaving the page. To add a comment, tap the Share button at the top-right of the Description page and select Facebook.

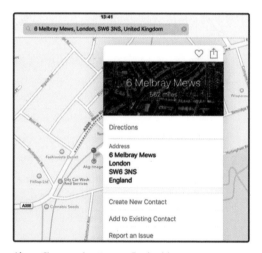

○ **Location:** In the Facebook Status Update box add your location by tapping the Check In icon in the bottom-left corner. Choose who you want to share it with by tapping the Friends icon and selecting from the list.

Above: Share your location over Facebook by tapping your location in the Maps app and choosing the Share button and then selecting Facebook.

Ask Siri to Update Your Friends

Siri can also update your Facebook status for you. Hold the Home button to launch Siri, say 'Post to Facebook' and dictate your message. Anything said after Facebook will be posted to your wall (iPad 3 and later).

Hot Tip

To keep up with what is happening on Facebook go to Settings, General, Notifications, Facebook and then turn on Allow Notifications.

TWITTER

The social networking and micro-blogging site, where every post is 140 characters or fewer, was the first to be fully integrated with the iPad. You can send a Tweet and add pictures or your location, without using the Twitter app.

Setting up Twitter

This is very similar to setting up Facebook. Go to Settings, Twitter. You can download and install the Twitter app, if you haven't already, although you can Tweet without it.

What you will need is a Twitter account. If you have one already, enter your details. If not, set one up here by tapping Create New Account. If, like many people, you have several accounts – one for your personal Tweets, another for a business or a hobby – then tap Add Account and enter the details. Now you are already signed in and ready to go, whether or not you use the standalone Twitter app.

Tweeting: Step-by-step

1. Simply tap the Twitter app to open it and click the Tweet box with a quill at the top of the screen. Your Twitter profile pic is already entered in the message box.

2. To send from a different account, if you have one, tap your profile pic and select the one you want from the list.

Step 1: When Tweeting, change between accounts by tapping the username box and selecting the relevant name from the drop down list.

3. As you enter your message, the number at the bottom-right shows how many of the available 140 characters remain. When finished, tap Send.

4. You can also ask Siri to 'Send a Tweet'. Siri will open a Tweet box and ask: 'OK, what \would you like your message to say?' Dictate your message, and when it's correct, say 'Send' (only available on iPad 3 and later).

Tweeting Photos and Your Location: Step-by-step

If you have a photo you must share with your Twitter followers, it's easy to do through your iPad.

1. In either Photos or the Camera app (if you have an iPad2 or later), select the image and tap the Share button, then Twitter.This opens the Tweet box, with the photo clipped to the side. As before, choose the account to send it from and add your message. Notice that the image (in fact it's the shortened URL of where the image is stored) takes up a number of characters and reduces the amount left for your message.

2. To add your location, tap the arrow and tap Enable to allow Twitter to share your location. It's shown on a map, once you're located. If you decide you don't want to share your location after all, select None.

3. Alternatively, simply Tweet your location from within Maps. Tap the pin marking your location, then select the Share button and choose Twitter.

Step 1: Tweet a photo by selecting an image from your Photos app, tapping the Share button, and choosing the Twitter option.

4. The message Your Name's Location is automatically added to the Tweet box. Delete this and add your own if you prefer. Again the character count is reduced because of the attached location information. Tap Send to post to Twitter.

Hot Tip

To be notified when you receive a direct message or mention in Twitter, tap Settings, Notifications, Twitter and slide the switch for Notification Centre to On.

Merge Contacts with Twitter

With Twitter built in to the system, you can merge your friends' Twitter usernames or avatars and pictures with your Contacts. Go to Settings, Twitter and tap the Update Contacts button. Now if you tap on a contact's Twitter name you have the option to send them a Tweet or see all their recent Tweets – without having to visit Twitter.

Using the Apps

There are many different apps on the iPad, from Tweetbot or Friendly to the Twitter and Facebook apps themselves, which offer a similar rich experience to the one you get online: you can send direct messages, find followers, see who's following you, add friends and so on. What the integration with iOS offers is convenience – now, when you come across something you want to share, you can do so with a couple of taps regardless of which app you're using.

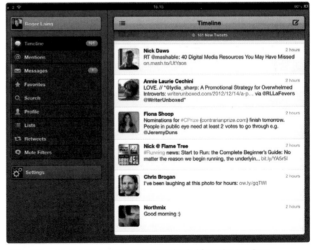

Above: Apps such as Tweetbot can be downloaded from the App Store if you want a more comprehensive Twitter experience which involves viewing trending hashtags, browsing your Twitter Feed, seeing who is following you, and sending direct messages.

LOCATION SERVICES

Whether it's forecasting the weather where you are or finding the nearest pizza restaurant, more and more apps are using the iPad's Location Services.

FIND YOURSELF

Location Services combine information from the iPad's built-in compass with Wi-Fi, mobile and GPS data to locate where you are.

Find My Friends: Step-by-step

Although the idea of tracking people is a little sinister, no one can be tracked without giving their permission.

1. Go to the App Store and download the free Find My Friends app (which installs as Find Friends).

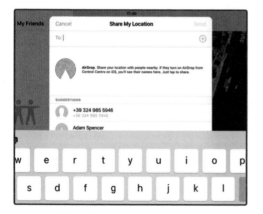

Above: Enter your contacts' names or email addresses or select them from the list to request them to share their location with you using the Find My Friends app.

2. Log in to the service using your Apple ID. Allow the app to Use your Current Location, and the compass arrow appears in the top bar.

3. Now ask your friends to share their location. Tap the Add button, type in their email address or contact name, if you allowed the app to access your Contacts, add your message and tap Send.

4. When your friend accepts, you can see their location but they can't see yours. To do so, they have to ask your permission. If they do, you'll see it under Requests.

5. Alternatively, you and your friends can tap to share locations with people nearby using AirDrop. Go to Control Centre (swipe up from any screen) and tap to switch it on. Friends' locations are marked with a purple dot. Your location is marked by a blue dot.

Temporary Sharing

This is great if you and your friends are planning to meet up for an evening. They can track you to make sure they go to the right location. This is now done through iMessages instead of Find Friends.

1. Start a conversation with the friend or group of friends you want to share your location with, then click Details.

2. Tap Send My Current Location to do that or tap Share My Location. In the box that opens up you can choose to share your location for an hour, until the end of the day or indefinitely.

EXPLORE WITH MAPS

The Maps app enables you to go local, and find the nearest restaurant or cinema, or international. It provides step-by-step directions and traffic conditions as well as a Flyover view and public transport directions for a limited number of major cities.

Getting Started with Maps

A Wi-Fi or mobile internet connection is needed for Maps to draw down the mapping information. It also relies on Location Services for many of its features. Make sure these are on by going to Settings, Privacy, and turning on Location Services and then Maps.

Hot Tip

On iPads with Wi-Fi and Cellular (3G and 4G), the built-in GPS will be used to determine your location more accurately, which can run down your battery faster.

Above: Activate Maps by making sure it is switched on to use Location Services.

Redrawing the World

Apple Maps was introduced with iOS 6 and has had a few teething problems, most notably misplacing several major cities. Apple has promised to improve the app but isn't likely to return to the previous version, based on Google maps, although that is still available on the original iPad.

Find a Location

1. Tap the Maps app, then type the name of the place you're looking for in the Search bar. You can search by geographic features, place names, neighbourhood names, street addresses, landmarks, business names and so on. In countries where the Nearby service is available tap the Search box to see a list of locations arranged by categories, such as Restaurants or Groceries.

2. If you're looking for somewhere close by, such as a coffee shop or theatre, tap the compass arrow to zoom in on your current location.

3. Maps will show locations on the map. Tap one that interests you to open an address bar. Tap the > icon to open the Info window.

4. This tells you more about the location and may include photos, reviews, directions to and from the location, or a link to the website. It also has options to add it to Contacts, share the location on Facebook and Twitter or bookmark it.

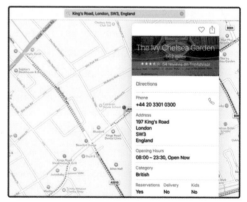

Change the View

Tap the information icon at the bottom-right corner of the screen and you can change the way you look at the location.

Above: Tap the > icon to open the Info window to find out more information about the location the pin is marking, including photos, reviews and directions. You can also share the location with others.

○ **Map**: This is the standard style.

○ **Transport**: Where this is available it shows public transport.

○ **Satellite**: This has overhead photographic views.

○ **3D**: Tap the 3DMap button to zoom in on the map and tilt it. If HD resolution satellite pictures are available for the location, the 3D button changes to a Flyover button.

Get Directions

To get directions to a location, by car, on foot or using public transport, tap the Directions button. Enter where you are and where you're going in the Start and End fields. Maps displays the route – and any alternatives – along with time and distance information.

Check Traffic En Route

Tap the information button in the bottom-right and you can see what road conditions are like (where the service is available). Orange dots mark slow moving traffic, red dots show stop-go driving, while other icons warn of roadworks and accidents.

Step-by-step Navigation

With the help of Siri, Maps offers step-by-step GPS navigation, similar to the sat-nav in a car or handheld system. It will also store maps of a very large surrounding area so you can still browse and use GPS navigation when you are outside Wi-Fi or mobile data coverage.

Above: Maps will display alternative routes to your destination, with times and distances noted.

Hot Tip

Let Siri be your travelling companion. Siri can find locations, tell you what points of interest or services are nearby and get directions for your trip (iPad 3 and above).

YOUR PHOTOS

The iPad is the complete photographer's kit – able to capture great photos, display them in their full beauty on a high-definition screen and store thousands of pictures in your own electronic album.

TAKE AMAZING PHOTOS

Cameras were first introduced with the iPad 2 and have been significantly upgraded since. As a hand-held camera, the iPad is bulky but with both a front and backward-facing lens, it can provide consistently good results.

	iPad				iPad Air		iPad Mini			iPad Pro	
	iPad 1	iPad 2	iPad 3	iPad 4	iPad Air	iPad Air 2	iPad Mini	iPad Minis 2 and 3	iPad Mini 4	12.9 inch iPad Pro	9.7 inch iPad Pro
Front camera	None	FaceTime	FaceTime HD	FaceTime HD			FaceTime HD			FaceTime HD	
Photos		0.3MP VGA Resolution	0.3MP VGA Resolution	1.2MP	1.2MP	1.2MP	1.2MP	1.2MP	1.2MP	1.2MP	5MP
Video		0.3MP VGA Resolution	0.3MP VGA Resolution	20p HD Video	720p HD Video	720p HD Video	720p HD Video	720p HD Video	720p HD Video	720p HD Video	720p HD Video
FaceTime		Wi-Fi	Wi-Fi + Cellular	Wi-Fi + Cellular	Wi-Fi + Cellular	Wi-Fi + Cellular	Wi-Fi + Cellular	Wi-Fi + Cellular	Wi-Fi + Cellular	Wi-Fi + Cellular	Wi-Fi + Cellular
Rear camera	None	Back camera	iSight	iSight	iSight	iSight	iSight	iSight	iSight	iSight	iSight
Photos		0.7MP	5MP	5MP	5MP	8MP	5MP	5MP	8MP	8MP	12MP
Video		720p HD Video	1080p HD Video	1080p HD Video	1080p HD Video	1080p HD Video	1080p HD Video	1080p HD Video	1080p HD Video	1080p HD Video	4K HD Video

Taking a Picture: Step-by-step

1. To take a picture, tap the Camera app and you should see the image. If you're in the picture, you're using the forward-pointing camera.

2. To switch to the rear camera, tap the camera icon with the curved arrows. Make sure that the mode is set to Photo and not Video or any of the other settings such as Time-lapse, Square or Panoramic.

Step 3: Tap anywhere on screen to focus on that part of the picture, as indicated by a white frame.

3. A rectangle briefly appears where the exposure is set. This is done automatically but you can adjust it manually. Tap the light icon next to the rectangle, then slide up or down to change it.

4. When using the rear camera, tap the image with two fingers together and push them apart to zoom in on the area you want to shoot. This also works in video on later iPads.

5. To help you frame your shot, you can also overlay a grid of thin white lines. To do so go to Settings, select Photos & Camera and slide the Grid switch to On.

6. When ready, take your shot by pressing the round button on the screen. Alternatively, you can use the up and down volume button on the side of the iPad.

7. The pictures you've taken can be viewed in the small square box in the bottom corner. Tap the image to bring up the controls, which are the same as those in the Photos app. These let you view, share and edit your images. Tap Done to return to the camera.

EDIT YOUR PHOTOS

However good or bad a photographer you are, the iPad's image-editing tools can make your pictures look better.

Photos App

It's all too easy, in the rush to capture a moment, to end up with a less than perfect photo. The Photos app (for iPad 2 and later) gives you the basic tools to make your pictures better – whether they are images taken with the iPad itself, streamed through iCloud or uploaded from your digital camera.

Hot Tip

After you save your edits you can still go back to the original, so don't worry if you make a change you wish you hadn't. Tap the image, then Edit and tap Revert.

○ **To start editing**: tap the Photos app with its easily recognizable sunflower icon.

○ **To Edit**: Select the photo you want to change, tap to view it and then tap the Edit button.

○ **Editing tools**: Buttons for the main editing tools appear on screen:

Above: Use the Pixelmator app to edit your photos by rotating, cropping, enhancing and removing red-eye from images.

1. **Auto-enhance**: the magic wand icon will adjust the colour and contrast of your image.

2. **Rotate and Crop**: This lets you alter the angle of the picture to straighten the image. You can also resize your pictures by tapping the Crop button and then pushing the corners of the grid that appears to adjust the frame.

3. **Photo Filters**: let you apply different colour effects, such as Mono or Chrome.

4. **Adjustments**: Sets light, colour and black-and-white options.

5. **Remove Red Eye**: Tap each eye that needs correcting.

○ **Save your changes**: Tap Done. If you don't like the results tap Cancel, then Discard Changes.

○ **Constrain**: If you're planning to print your photos, you can constrain the crop ratios to match. Simply press the Constrain button at the bottom and select the proportions you want.

ADVANCED PHOTO EDITING

Make your pictures as eye-catching as possible, with iPad apps that offer the sort of sophisticated editing techniques usually found on more powerful computers.

Pixelmator App

Pixelmator provides advanced editing tools that are simple and effective to use on the iPad. It also supports Apple's Handoff feature, which means you can start editing on your iPad and then transfer the photo to the Mac and carry on right where you left off (or vice versa).

○ **Pixelmator**: Buy and install Pixelmator from the App Store, then tap to open. To start you need an image. You can import one from iCloud or the Photos app or take a photo with the iPad camera.

○ **Import an image**: Tap the + sign in the corner of the screen, then either tap Photos or iCloud Drive and follow the prompts.

○ **Create a new image**: Tap the + sign then Create Image. Tap Show Categories to see the available templates you can use, from collages to posters.

Hot Tip

If your images from iCloud Drive aren't showing up you need to set it up. Go to Settings, iCloud, iCloud Drive and turn on Pixelmator.

Above: Use the Pixelmator's editing tools to transform photos by altering properties and adding effects.

Above: With the Effects tool you can simply retouch photos or turn them into artistic creations.

○ **To take a photo:** Tap the + sign then Take Photo. Point at what you want to shoot. If you like the image tap Use Photo.

Editing Photos with Pixelmator

Once you've selected the photo you want to edit, tap the paint brush icon to open the photo-editing menu.

○ **Select Crop:** Do you want to cut some of the noise out of your photo? Using the grid you can focus in on the detail that's important, while keeping the aspect ratio the same. To change it click Undo or Revert to Original.

○ **Select retouch:**

1. **Repair:** lets you remove unwanted elements.

2. **Lighten or Darken:** Change areas of an image according to your preferences.

3. **Clone:** Copy part of the image from one area to another.

4. **Sharpen or Soften:** Change the focus on the photo to make it clearer or more blurred in different places.

5. **Fix red-eyes:** Easily and quickly get rid of red-eyes.

6. **Saturate or Desaturate:** Alter colour strength.

- **Effects**: Want to age your photo or make it more artistic? Tap Add Effects and swipe your finger through the thumbnails to choose which option to apply.

Applying Edits

With several of the tools, you tap and hold the area of the image where you want to apply the change, then move the circle to increase or decrease the effect.

Other Photo-editing Apps

There are many excellent photo-editing apps available from third-party developers. Among them are Adobe Photoshop Fix for retouching photos and Snapseed, which saves over the original photo rather than duplicate it to make it easier to revert to the original image.

ORGANIZING YOUR PHOTOS

Arranging your images in albums makes it easier to find the ones you want and show them off.

Create Photo Albums: Step-by-step

You can use the built-in Photos app to set up your albums on iPad 2 and later.

1. Tap to open, then select Albums and tap the + sign in the top-left corner. In the New Album box enter a name, then tap Save.

2. The Photos view shows all the images on your iPad. Scroll through and select the images you want to add to that album. As you select each one, it is marked with a blue tick in the lower-right corner. Tap Done to add the photos to the new album.

Step 1: Create a new album by selecting the + sign from the album screen and entering the name into the New Album box.

3. If you already have an album and want to add more images to it, open the album, then tap the Photos button for a view of all your images and press select. Choose the photos you want, as above, and tap the Add To button.

4. Alternatively, tap the Photos button, press Select, choose your photos, press Add To and scroll through the albums to find where you want to place them.

Smart Albums

Some albums are automatically created for you. So you'll see there are albums for the latest selfies, screenshots, photo bursts and panoramas.

Manage Your Albums

When viewing your album list tap Edit. To delete an album tap the X in the corner or to rearrange the order touch the album and drag it to another location in the list.

Above: Photos has a new tab in iOS 10 called Memories, which create slideshows of your photos, such as 'Best of Last 3 Months'.

ADDING EFFECTS

From stretching and twisting your face to creating your own comic book images, there is a range of apps to add special effects to your photos.

Fun with Photo Booth

This works with either the front or rear camera. Tap to open Photo Booth and choose the effect you want. Depending on the one you choose, you can pinch, swipe or rotate the image to alter the intensity of the effect.

1. Tap the camera to take the shot, which will be preceded by white flash. The picture appears in the photo roll at the bottom of the screen.

2. Tap the picture, then the Share button and you have a range of options to email, copy, print or save it to online storage accounts like Dropbox.

Instagram

The photo-sharing app has been a massive hit with iPhone users since it launched. It lets you take a photo, choose a filter to change its look and feel, then post it to Instagram for friends and family to view. Surprisingly, though, given the iPad's superior screen, there's no native iPad app, so you have to use the iPhone version.

Add Text to Your Photos

Remember the Polaroid instant camera with the thick white border around the images that you could write on? Instant app recreates the Polaroid effect and even includes different handwriting fonts for adding your text.

Comic Book Effect

Create your own comic strip with ComicBook! It turns you and your friends into stars of your own comic book in seconds, and you can publish direct to Facebook.

Other Effects

There are iPad-specific apps to add virtually any effect you can think of – from vintage film-star looks to pop art – and then combine them in unusual ways to create collages, moodboards, posters and the like.

Above: Photo Booth allows you to alter an image in many different ways by choosing various effects.

VIEWING PHOTOS

The iPad's display is great for showing off your photos, and if you have one with the Retina screen, they'll look even better.

PHOTO DISPLAYS

The iPad is a wonderfully portable digital photo album that can deliver slide shows or be an electronic picture frame that can change photos automatically.

Album Photos

1. Open Photos, tap the Albums button, and you'll see various ones listed. These also correspond to any picture folders you sync from your computer.

2. Tap on the album, and you'll see all the individual photos. Tap on any photo to view it up close. Tap the album name in the top-left to return to a view of all the photos.

3. Tap Albums at the top-left corner to return to the list of albums.

4. Alternatively, put a finger at the top and bottom of the screen and pinch them together to pull the photos back into album view.

Hot Tip

Retina is just Apple's marketing term to convey the extraordinary quality of screens with a high pixel density, where the average human retina can't make out individual pixels when seen from a normal viewing distance.

Step 2: Tap on any individual photo in your album to view it close up.

Slideshow

To make more of your photos, add music and fancy transition effects to create a slide show.

1. In Photos, select the album or group of photos you want then press the Slideshow button.

2. Tap the first picture and press the pause button while you select the effects you want.

Step 3: Select slideshow options such as the theme for the transitions and music.

3. Tap options. Themes lets you change the transitions between slides, while Music allows you to choose from the preset sounds or access your iTunes music. You also have options to repeat the slideshow and change the speed it plays at.

4. Tap the Play button to start the Slideshow again. To stop the slideshow, tap anywhere and press the pause button.

Picture Frame

Apps like Picmatic can turn your iPad into a digital photo frame.

1. Open Picmatic and tap the screen to show the settings menu.

2. Tap the cog wheel and under Photo Display select what kind of frame you want. This includes the Layout, the number of images in each screen and whether there's a frame or any filter effects.

3. Under Albums select which one you want to use. Scroll to Photo Transition and you can set how the images change, how quickly and how long they're displayed, as well as the order in which the photos appear. You can also add time and date to the display.

Hot Tip

If the picture frame is on public display, you might not want that photo of you asleep in a deck chair popping up. To avoid this, create your own photo album specifically for use with Picmatic.

4. To prevent notifications from other apps appearing on top of your pictures you need to temporarily restrict use of the iPad to Picmatic while it's running. Click on Lock App Instructions and follow the detailed information to set it up.

5. Tap the music icon to add sounds to the photo display. When you've finished tap the screen once to hide the Settings bar and you have your digital photo frame.

Deleting Photos

However embarrassing a photo is, it may not be possible to delete it from the iPad. You can only delete photos you've taken on the iPad, that have been uploaded via the camera connection kit, saved from your email or a website using Safari, or are in your Photo Stream.

○ **To delete a single photo**: Tap the photo you want to delete, then the dustbin icon and press the red Delete Photo button. If the photo is in your iCloud Photo Library it will be deleted from all your devices.

Above: Delete groups of photos by tapping the Select button and choosing the photos to delete. Each one will be marked with a blue tick. Once you have finished selecting, tap the Delete button.

○ **To delete a group of photos**: Tap the Select button followed by each photo you want to delete. Those selected are marked with a tick. Tap the Delete button, then confirm by pressing the Delete Photos button.

○ **No delete option**: In some albums there is no delete option, as these photos are copies of images synced with your computer. To delete them, go to your computer and remove the photos from any albums that sync with the iPad.

SHOW PHOTOS ON A BIGGER SCREEN

The iPad screen uses a special technology – In-Plane Switching (IPS) – for better viewing from different angles. However, for a bigger display, wirelessly transmit your photos to other screens, such as your TV.

Mirror Your Pictures with AirPlay

To do this, you'll need a second generation Apple TV or later. Despite its name, it is not a TV but a receiver that connects to your TV with a high-definition cable. Special AirPlay wireless technology mirrors what's on your iPad to the receiver, which displays it on your TV.

- **To connect successfully** you need an iPad 2 or later, and both your Apple TV and iPad have to be on the same wireless network.

- **To show off your photos**, open Photos, tap Albums and then select the one you want to display. Tap on the photo, then the Share icon and select AirPlay (a square screen with an upward-pointing arrow at its base).

Above: Use AirPlay to show your photos on Apple TV by tapping on a selected photo, selecting the Share icon, then Airplay and the Apple TV option.

- **Select Apple TV** and your photo will appear on the TV screen. You can flick between images, zoom in, pause and move from landscape to portrait view, and the changes will be reflected on the big screen.

Physically Connect Your iPad Display and TV

An alternative way to mirror what's on your iPad screen to a TV or other display is through a physical connection. You'll need an Apple Digital AV adapter or VGA adapter. Plug this into your iPad and then connect it to an High Density Multimedia Interface (HDMI) cable from the TV or other display.

ADDING PHOTOS

There are numerous ways to put photos onto the iPad to take advantage of its high-quality display.

SAVED PHOTOS

Whether it's direct from the camera, if you have a camera-equipped iPad, or images from the web, you can save them all to the Photos app.

Add Photos with the Camera

Photos taken with the iPad appear automatically in the All Photos album if you use iCloud Photo Library. If you don't they will appear in the Camera Roll album instead. You can access them directly by tapping the square icon in the bottom-left of the Camera app.

Hot Tip

If you use Photo Booth to apply special effects to your photos, these will also appear in the Camera Roll/All Photos album.

Add Photos from Other Apps

○ **Safari:** As you browse the web, you'll come across images you want to save. Tap and hold the image you want. In the box that opens, select Save Image and it will be downloaded to Photos.

○ **Messages:** Tap the image you've been sent to open it full-size then tap again and select the Share button in the top-right corner and select Save Image.

Above: To download a photo from Safari, tap and hold the image and then select the Save Image option.

- **Email**: Select the email with the image attached. Tap and hold the image in the email then select Save Image from the pop-up box.

Screenshots

Want to capture an image of what's on your iPad screen – such as your highest ever score on a favourite game? Press the Sleep/Wake button at the top of the iPad and the Home button at the same time then release. There'll be a flash of white light, a camera click and the image will appear in your Camera Roll. This is how the screenshots for this book were taken.

UPLOADED PHOTOS

To transfer photos direct from your digital camera, you need a separate adapter. Alternatively, upload them first to your computer and use one of a growing number of third-party apps to transfer them wirelessly to the iPad.

Camera Connection Kit

This kit, available from Apple, fits the iPad's original 30-pin dock connector design. It is one of the few ways you can upload photos (and videos) direct from your camera. Each kit contains two adapters: one for the USB cable from your camera, the other for a Secure Digital (SD) memory card. Later iPads with the Lightning connector can use the Lightning to SD Card Camera Reader.

Above: Download photos directly from your digital camera using an SD memory card connection kit.

Importing Photos with the Adapters

Once you've made the physical connection, open Photos, if it hasn't already opened automatically.

1. Tap individual photos to select them, then press Import. To upload all the photos, tap Import All.

2.   Tap the photos you want to transfer, touch the red sync button and select where you want your photos to be transferred to/from.

3.   In Photos, tap Albums, Last Import to see the photos.

Step 1: Download the PhotoSync app to transfer photos to your iPad from other devices wirelessly.

Wireless Transfer

There are several apps, such as PhotoSync, used here, which let you wirelessly transfer your photos to the iPad from either your computer or other iDevices. PhotoSync will sync your images with online photo storage sites, such as Flickr, Dropbox and Facebook. It can transfer from one to a thousand pictures at a time.

1.   Install the app on the iPad and any other iOS device you are using, as well as your Mac or PC.

2.   Go to Settings, Privacy, Location Services (just Location Services on iPad 1) and turn on for PhotoSync, so the app can access your photo library.

3.   Transfer your photos directly using the Wi-Fi network or Bluetooth, or via your web browser.

SYNCED PHOTOS

To make sure you have all your latest photos on the iPad, sync your photos using iTunes or automatically download the most recent shots via iCloud.

My Photo Stream

This links up all your iOS devices or computers running iCloud so you can share any photos automatically using My Photo Stream.

1. My Photo Stream should be turned on by default. If not, go to Settings, iCloud, Photos and switch on Upload to My Photo Stream. Now if you take a photo on your iPad, it will appear in all others that have My Photo Stream running.

2. The My Photo Stream album stores 1,000 of your most recent photos on iCloud for 30 days.

3. Remember to move them from here to another album, share them or delete them before they are replaced as part of the normal rotation of photos.

iTunes

Traditionally, the main way to add photos is to sync them through iTunes (although you can't do this if you turn on iCloud Photo Library).

Step 2: Check Sync Photos and then choose the library you wish to sync with.

1. Connect your iPad to the computer, via USB cable or wirelessly, and click iTunes. Your iPad will show in the top bar. Click this and select Photos.

2. Make sure there's a check mark beside Sync Photos, then click on the drop-down menu to choose your picture library, such as Photos.

3. It's unlikely that you'll want to sync all your photos tor have sufficient space. So click Selected albums and Automatically include photos from the period of time you want. Then go through the list of Albums and select the ones to sync.

4. When finished, click Apply or Sync.

Hot Tip

As you select each photo album, keep an eye on the Capacity bar underneath. This will change, indicating how big it is and the amount of free space left.

SHARING PHOTOS

The iPad is a great digital hub for collecting, managing and adding special effects to your photos before sharing them online.

iCLOUD PHOTO LIBRARY

Copy your photos to Apple's online storage service, iCloud, and they can be automatically pushed out and received wirelessly on your computer (Mac and PC) and iOS devices. To turn on iCloud Photo Library go to Settings, iCloud, Photos. To set up iCloud, *see* page 52.

iCloud Photo Sharing

Create albums of photos to share with your friends and family.

Hot Tip

iCloud provides unlimited free storage for music and apps, etc. that you buy through iTunes, as well as for your My Photo Stream. However, there's only 5GB of free storage for your documents, Mail, iCloud Photo Library and backups, although you can purchase more space as needed.

Step 1: Activate iCloud Photo Sharing by toggling the switch to On in the Photos section of iCloud settings.

1. First, tap Settings, then iCloud and turn on iCloud Photo Sharing.

2. Open the Photos app, then the Select button. Select the photo(s) you want to show off to others (blue ticks will indicate those selected) and tap the Share button in the top-left corner.

3. Tap iCloud Photo Sharing, add any comments you have, then share to an existing shared album, if there is one, or select a new one.

4. You can invite people to view your shared album using their email address (or the mobile phone number they use for iMessage).

5. If your contacts use iOS 7 or OS X Mavericks or later, they can add their own photos and videos.

6. Alternatively, you can publish your album to a website for anyone to view. To do so select the shared album, tap People then turn on Public Website. Tap Share Link to announce the site.

SHARING DIRECT FROM YOUR iPAD

To make it easier to share your photos, via text, email or social media, all the different options have been brought together under one Share button.

Photos App

There are several ways to share images from the built-in Photos app. Tap to open it, select the image to share and press the Share button – a square box with pointing arrow.

- **Mail**: Tap this to open a new email message with the photo already attached. Tap Images to select the size of image you want to send.

- **Message**: Again, the photo is automatically added to your message. All you need do is add the contact address, your message and press Send.

- **iCloud Photo Sharing**: Press this to add an individual photo to shared albums stored on iCloud.

Above: Share your photos by tapping the Share icon in the top right corner. Choose how you want to share your image from the options shown, which include sharing via Facebook, Twitter and Email.

- **Facebook**: Posting a photo to the world's biggest social network is also incredibly easy. Tap the Facebook icon and the picture is already attached. Tap the album icon at the bottom to choose the name of the Facebook album to which the photo will be added.

- **Twitter**: Tap the icon and a tweet box opens with a thumbnail of the photo attached by a paper clip. Notice that the number of characters left for your message has been reduced from the normal 140. This is to allow for the link to the page where the image will be stored.

ONLINE ALBUMS

Move your pictures from the iPad to online photo-sharing sites such as Flickr and Google's Picasa or create your own web gallery using Journals.

Above: The Picasa Web Albums HD app lets you access your Picasa photo library online, and and post photos to Google+.

Picasa

As well as being an online photo-sharing site in its own right, Picasa, which is owned by Google, is also used to create the photo albums in Google's social network, Google+. There are third-party apps, such as Web Albums HD, which let you access your entire Picasa photo library online, as well as post to Google+.

Flickr

As it's one of the biggest online photo-sharing sites, several photo-editing apps, such as Photos, let you post directly to Flickr. In addition, there is a Flickr app as well as many third-party apps, such as FlickStackr, for bringing Flickr photo-sharing to the iPad. Typically these allow you to upload and download photos, add information and view Flickr groups.

> *Hot Tip*
>
> **If you want to set up and view albums only on Google+ itself, there is a Google+ app available in iTunes.**

PHOTO SERVICES

Get creative with your iPad and use your photos to create online journals, greeting cards and much more.

Journals

With apps like Day One, you can create your own photo journal and diary capturing your life as you live it. All your memories and photos can be synced through through iCloud or Dropbox or via the Day One Mac desktop application.

Photobooks

Apps such as eBook Magic take your photos – including pictures taken with your iPad camera – and turn them into photo albums, story books for your children or travel journals.

Greeting Cards

Surprise gran with a greeting card featuring the family. Apps such as Greetings Studio let you incorporate photos from the iPad into a series of templates to create personalized cards for all occasions.

Above: Turn your photos into jigsaw puzzles by downloading the Jigsawed Jigsaw Puzzle app.

Calendars

Make your holiday last a year. InstaCalendar for the iPad will let you memorialize your trip by turning your travel shots – or any photo – into a calendar.

Puzzles

Jigsawed Jigsaw Puzzle turns your photos into jigsaws – ranging from 9 pieces if it's for the children to 324 for the more experienced.

YOUR VIDEOS

Shooting and editing video is so easy on the iPad that you will soon be creating movie clips to share on the internet. Go viral, and your clip could be the latest online sensation.

VIDEO RECORDING

Point and tap is all you need to do to start recording your video, provided you've got an iPad 2 or later, but there are a few things to bear in mind in order to get the best results.

Shooting Video

The video recorder is built in to the Camera app you use to take photos.

1. To start, simply tap the Camera app and rotate the camera options until Video is highlighted in yellow.

2. Point the camera at the scene you want to capture and tap the recording button in the centre-right of the screen.

3. As recording starts the red circle changes to a square. A timer with flashing red dot showing how long you've been recording appears on the right-hand side.

4. To finish recording, tap the record button again. Watch your movie clip by tapping the video library icon in the bottom corner.

Step 2: Start recording your video by tapping the red recording button to the centre-right of the screen.

Focusing Your Video Recording

While the iPad has its own autofocus, you can target a particular area. Tap the screen on the area you want to focus on and the iPad will make the necessary adjustments.

Which Video Camera to Use

The iPad has come with two cameras since the iPad 2.

○ **The front-facing camera**: Primarily intended for FaceTime video chat calls, this has a lower resolution than the rear camera. If you do want to use the front camera – perhaps to introduce your clip – switch lenses by tapping the camera icon with two circular arrows on the bottom menu.

○ **The rear camera**: The default one for video. The iPad 2 has a 0.7-megapixel lens that shoots video at 720p. On later iPads this iSight camera was upgraded, to a 5-megapixel lens as standard with 8-megapixels on the top end models. These later iPads shoot 1080p HD video and have auto-stabilization features to compensate for shakiness when filming.

Hot Tip

Although you can view your video equally well in portrait or landscape mode, choose one or the other before you begin and don't switch midway through filming.

EDITING VIDEO

Tidy up your video by using the Camera app to trim unwanted footage from the beginning and end of your clip – or use iMovie for more extensive movie-editing.

Simple Editing

1. Once you've shot your video, tap the Camera Roll in the bottom corner to view the clip or select one previously recorded from your videos album in Photos and tap Edit.

Step 2: Tap the screen to show a timeline of your video, with the cursor marking where you are in the clip.

Step 4: Drag the yellow trim handles to shorten or lengthen the video clip.

Hot Tip
It's best to have your iPad in horizontal view when running iMovie as you can see more of your timeline and the editing controls.

2. When the video opens you'll see there's a scrubbing bar at the bottom – that is a timeline of your video, with the cursor showing where you are in the clip.

3. Tap the video clip and a yellow outline box appears with a thick border – trim handle – at either end.

4. Dragging either yellow trim handle will shorten or lengthen the clip.

5. When you have the section of the video that you want to keep, tap the Done button.

6. If you try to increase the clip's length but the trim handle doesn't move, it means there are no additional frames to add.

More Advanced Movie Editing
With Apple's iMovie app (available from the App Store) on the iPad, you have many of the useful video-editing features that are available in the full version of the program that runs on your computer.

Import Video
The iMovie app lets you polish up your video footage, combine clips, and add titles and special effects in the transitions between scenes.

1. Open iMovie, tap the + button, then New Project to create a new folder for your video.

2. Grant iMovie permission to access your photos. To add other videos, tap the filmstrip icon, where you should see the most recent video clip you recorded. Tap this and then the blue downward-pointing arrow to add it to your timeline.

3. Tap the Photos icon to access your photo library. As well as any video clips you have, you can also add photos. In fact, several copies of the photo are added so that it lasts on screen for about three to six seconds. There are also slight variations to give the effect that the camera is zooming in on the scene. Tap the photo you want, and it will be added to the end of the timeline.

Step 3: Add a photo from your photo library to the end of your timeline. Multiple copies are added so the photo lasts on screen.

4. Alternatively, capture video direct from within iMovie by tapping the video camera icon. This accesses the iPad's iSight camera and you can shoot your HD video as before.

5. The white vertical line, known as the playhead, shows where you are in the video. The image by the playhead is displayed in the preview window above.

6. Flick your finger left or right to scroll through the timeline. Pinch your fingers to zoom in and out or press the triangular Play button under the preview window to start the video.

Edit Video

Having added the video clips to your project, you can edit them into your personal blockbuster movie.

- **Rearrange a clip:** To change the order in which they play, tap-and-hold the clip you're moving and drag it to the new location. The existing clips move to make space.

- **Delete a clip:** Double-tap the clip you want to remove, and tap Delete in the bottom corner. If you change your mind and want to add it back, it will still be in the list of available video clips.

Above: Delete a clip by double-tapping and selecting Delete.

- **Trim a clip:** This is done in much the same way as in the Camera app. Tap the clip in the timeline and then drag the yellow endpoints to a new start and finish position.

- **Split a clip:** Tap the clip you want, and drag it until the playhead is right over the spot where you want to split it. Tap the video, and it will be outlined in yellow. Swipe your finger down the playhead as though you were slicing it in half. Now you can add another clip or insert a different transition.

Edit Transitions

The on-screen move from one clip to the next is called a transition. There are three types.

- **Cut transition:** Marked by a white line on a black square this is called None in iMovie because, although there is a break between clips, there's no transition effect. On screen, one clip will just flow into the next but the transition will still be shown in the timeline in case you want to change it.

- **Theme transition:** Marked by two white boxes on a black background. To choose the theme to apply, tap the Project Settings button – the cog wheel – in the top-right corner and make your choice.

○ **Action transitions**: Move from one clip or photo to another using one of the Dissolve, Slide, Wipe or Fade effects.

Select Transitions

By default, there's a transition between each video clip and photo in the project.

1. To change it, double-tap the transition icon in the timeline.

2. From the Transition Settings that open below select the style you want. To change how long it lasts, tap the duration required.

3. Tap on the yellow triangles below the transition button to open the precision editor. This lets you move the endpoints where you want the transition to begin and end. Tap the triangles to return to the timeline.

Hot Tip

If Cross-Dissolve isn't available, it's because the clips either side aren't long enough to support it.

Step 3: Tap the yellow triangles below the transition button to open the precision editor.

Add Titles

Another way to give a more professional finish to your videos is to overlay titles.

1. Double-tap the clip and select Title from the bar that appears below. Boxes showing the different styles appear above.

2. Tap your chosen text style and use the on-screen keyboard to add your title.

3. On some themes you can add a location. Tap Location and enter the details.

ADDING SOUND TO YOUR VIDEO

From recording your own commentary to adding a song from your iTunes collection, there are several ways to add sound to your video.

Background Music

If you are adventurous, you can record your own music with an app like GarageBand; you can also select iMovie theme music or add any song from your iTunes library.

1. To turn Theme music on tap the Project Settings button (gear wheel icon) in the upper-right of the screen and select the appropriate option.

2. To add music, tap the Audio button (musical notes icon), then Theme Music.

3. Only one music track can play at a time. If you add a music track when there is already one in place, it will play after

Step 1: Tap the musical notes icon and select Theme Music to begin adding background music to your videos.

this if the video is long enough. If it's not it will replace the original music.

4. If you have background music looping turned on (that is the track keeps repeating throughout the video) then you can only have one track.

5. To set the volume of the background music tap the Waveform button in the middle bar and you'll see a mix of yellow and red peaks. Red shows the audio is too loud and likely to be distorted.

6. Change the volume until these peaks disappear, by double-tapping the green background in the timeline that represents the audio clip and adjusting the slider.

Sound Effects

Add these at relevant points by scrolling through the timeline so the playhead is where you want to add the sound effect. Tap the Audio button and then Sound effects. Preview a sound by tapping the Play button on the right. It will be shown as a blue bar in the timeline. Adjust the volume by double-tapping this and then moving the slider.

Backing Track

When you record the video, it might include all sorts of background noises or conversations. If the clip does have its own audio, iMovie will automatically lower the volume (known as audio ducking) of the background music.

Voiceover

Place the playhead where you want to start recording and then tap the microphone icon.

Step 5: Set the volume of your background music by tapping the Waveform button and using the slider to change the volume until any red peaks disappear.

Above: After recording your voiceover you can choose whether to review it, retake it, cancel it or accept it.

Tap Record in the pop-up box and after a three-second countdown, start talking. Press the Stop button to finish recording. You then have the options to Review the voiceover, Retake, Cancel or Accept it.

SHARE YOUR VIDEOS

Once you have the perfect movie, the iPad makes it simple to share your video with friends, family or the wider world of the internet, via YouTube and Facebook.

Sharing from Photos

Go to the Videos folder in Photos, select the clip you want, tap the Share button and choose your preferred option.

- **Email:** There will be a slight delay while the video is compressed to reduce the size of the file that's sent. Because this also reduces the quality of the video, do not use email to send the video to your computer – it's better to sync them using iTunes.

- **Message:** The video is automatically attached, so you just have to add who it's going to and write your message.

- **YouTube:** This is the best option to display your video properly. Enter your sign-in details in the pop-up box and then add a title, description, tags and category for your video.

Sharing from iMovie

1. When you've finished, tap Done and you'll return to the Home screen. If you haven't given the project a name, do so now. Tap My Project and enter the title you prefer. Tap the Share button and you'll see the range of options available.

Hot Tip

By default your video is uploaded in standard definition. Select HD if you want high definition. As the file size is much bigger, it will take longer to upload, so you should only do this over a Wi-Fi connection to the internet rather than mobile.

2. Most links are to well-known video-sharing sites, such as YouTube, Facebook and Vimeo. You will need to have an account for the site you select before you can upload your video.

3. The procedure is typically the same: enter your login details and then complete the form for your video. It should include a title, a description and the category under which it should be displayed. In addition you can choose the file size.

4. Some sites also let you set who can see the video through the privacy settings. There may be some videos that you want to share only with the family or friends, but, generally, if you want your video to be seen, it's best to go public.

5. You can also send your video to iCloud Photo Sharing or add it to iTunes, for syncing with your Mac or PC.

Step 1: Tap the Share button in the iMovie Home screen to view and select how you want to share your video from the options shown.

Hot Tip

If you do go public on a video-sharing site, make sure you have the permission of anyone featured in it and you have copyright for the material used.

ENTERTAINMENT CENTRE

Whether it's a Hollywood blockbuster or must-see TV series, it can be bought or rented to view in glorious detail on your iPad – or to project onto your TV.

AIRPLAY

AirPlay lets you wirelessly transmit videos and other content from your iPad to the big screen – and show them on your TV.

Apple TV

As well as streaming what's on your iPad – music, photos and so on – Apple TV also lets you show content on the big screen from Netflix, YouTube and Vimeo, plus films and TV shows from the iTunes store and more.

Above: The Apple TV black box connects to your TV and wirelessly receives video streams from your iPad.

1. To mirror the screen of your iPad on the TV wirelessly, you will need the second generation Apple TV or later and an iPad 2 or later. This black box is physically connected to your TV by High Density Multimedia Interface (HDMI) cable and wirelessly receives the video stream from your iPad, using AirPlay mirroring.

2. Turn on AirPlay on your Apple TV. Using the remote supplied with it, navigate the on-screen display on your TV and select Settings, Airplay and turn it on. It's easier with the fourth-generation TV and the Siri Remote which has touch and voice control for the TV.

3. Swipe up from the bottom edge of your iPad to open the Control Center.

4. Select AirPlay and then tap the Apple TV you want to use to mirror the iPad.

Physical Connection to Your TV

For a less flexible approach to mirroring what's on your iPad screen to a TV or other display, you can cable the two together.

Step 3: Open the Control Center, tap the AirPlay icon and then select Apple TV.

View Rented Movies through Apple TV

Once Apple TV is set up, you should see the iTunes Store, which lets you access the same video and TV shows available through the iPad.

1. Select Movies from the main Apple TV menu. Browse through the different options – top movies, new releases, Genius recommendations, film genres or individual titles. You can also search by title if you have a film in mind.

2. When you see a movie you want to rent, select it. With the second-generation Apple TV and later it will default to the high-definition version of the film (which will take longer to download and will be more expensive).

3. To change this preference go to Settings, iTunes store, then Video Resolution and change from the two HD formats 1080p or 720p to Standard Definition (SD). In fact, the 1080p movies will only play on the third generation Apple TV.

4. A confirmation message will appear on screen. Click OK if you want to continue, and the film will download. A message appears when it is ready to view. Press Play to start watching.

5. If you rent a movie through Apple TV, it can be viewed only through Apple TV.

Buy and Rent Videos through the iTunes Store

1. Tap the iTunes store app and select Films at the bottom.

2. You can select from Featured movies, which shows you the most popular films to rent or buy, as well as recommendations from iTunes. Alternatively, select the Top Charts button and then the Films tab and you can see the most popular movies in each category.

3. By default, all types of movie are shown in both the Featured and Charts section. If you have a specific taste in film, such as horror, tap the Genres button and make your selection – then, just those movies will be shown.

Above: Select the Film tab at the bottom of the iTunes app to view movies available for renting and purchase.

4. When you see a movie you want to rent, select it. You'll see Details of the film, including a trailer, synopsis and cast list. At the top is the overall rating from iTunes users and the price to buy or rent the movie.

5. To see more detailed opinions about the film – and add your own once you've seen it – tap the Reviews tab.

6. If it doesn't appeal, select Related and you'll see similar films that

customers who purchased the film you're looking at have also bought.

7. Tap the Rent button if you want to hire the movie. You'll have up to 30 days to view the film. But once you've started to watch it, you have just 24 hours to complete it.

8. Movies rented through the iPad can be viewed only on the iPad (or on the TV using AirPlay). They can't be transferred to your computer for viewing there.

9. To buy a film, select the relevant button. For the iPad 3 and later, the default is to download the HD (high-definition) version of the movie. For the iPad 1 and 2 it will be the SD (standard-definition) version.

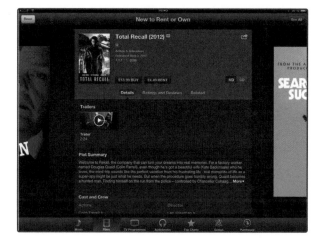

Above: Click on a movie you are interested in to see further details and the price to buy or rent.

Hot Tip

The HD version is more expensive and a much bigger file size, so will take longer to download.

Hot Tip

Don't worry if you accidentally delete a TV show or movie you have bought. Go to Purchased, select Films or TV Series and locate the programme you want to re-download.

TV Shows

TV shows operate in a similar way to the movies, except they are only available to buy. You can browse by Featured Programmes and Charts, and within each section you have the option to view single Episodes of a show or the collected Series. There are also an increasing number of TV

PLAY VIDEOS

Whether it's for the latest movie, a music clip or a converted file of the children's school play, the iPad is an immensely powerful video player.

MASTER VIDEO PLAYER

All the video content downloaded from the iTunes store – whether it's a movie, TV show or music video – appears automatically in the Videos app. Its distinctive icon features a movie clapperboard.

Playback

1. Turn your iPad to switch between viewing your video in portrait or widescreen (landscape) mode.

2. Tap the Play button (forward-facing triangle) or the video itself to start playback. Press the centre button to pause playback.

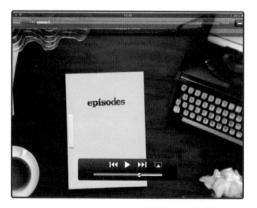

Step 4: Navigate to your chosen point in a video by dragging your finger to move the playhead along the timeline at the top of the screen.

3. Touch and hold the Rewind or Fast Forward icon to speed backward and forward through the video.

4. Alternatively, drag the playhead along the scrubber bar (as the video timeline is called) at the top to any point of the video you want.

5. As you drag the playhead back, slide your finger down the screen to slow the scrub rate. You'll see a label that reads Hi-Speed Scrubbing, Half-Speed Scrubbing and Fine Scrubbing.

6. To go right back to the beginning of the video, drag the playhead all the way to the left or simply tap the Rewind button (if the video has no chapters; if it does, it will go back to the beginning of the chapter).

7. Tap the Chapters button and you'll see a list of chapters in the movie (if there are any). Tap the name to go directly to that chapter.

8. Use the volume slider to raise or lower the soundtrack on the video.

9. To stop the video before it finishes playing, tap the Done button or press the Home button.

OTHER VIDEO PLAYERS

In addition to the Videos app, you can watch video on your iPad through the Safari web browser and third-party apps that connect directly to video sites.

Hot Tip

Want to know what videos are available online? OVGuide (www.ovguide.com) is an independent guide that includes free full length movies, TV shows, trending viral videos and clips.

Above: Access the OVGuide website to see what videos are available to view online.

Video Browsing

Browse the internet and you'll see that many websites, from personal blogs to international newspapers, music and entertainment sites, include video. Virtually any video in the standard MP4 format will play on the iPad through the Safari web browser.

As with all Apple devices running iOS, no Flash videos can play on the iPad directly. The popularity of the iPad is such that this is becoming less of an issue than it was before.

Rather than lose a portion of their audience, many sites are changing the format for their videos so they can run on the iPad. There are also browsers, like Skyfire, that do this conversion in the background so Flash videos will play on the iPad. It doesn't have a 100 per cent success rate, though.

Video Apps

There are several video sites that have their own apps for the iPad. Netflix and LOVEFiLM both have apps for subscribers to their service, as do Amazon and Hulu in the US with its Instant Video app. Typically, for a monthly subscription you can access any of the vast library of movies and TV shows these sites hold.

Video-sharing Sites

The popularity of YouTube was such that their app was built-in to the iPad's operating system, but Apple removed the YouTube app in iOS 6.

Instead, there is a standalone app, which you can download from the App Store. Another popular video-sharing site, Vimeo, has its own dedicated app for the iPad, while Maker (Maker.tv) offers professionally made shows that run as 'web series', viewable through Safari on the iPad.

TV Sites

Many TV companies have developed apps – such as BBC iPlayer and Sky Go – that let you watch programmes on the iPad, sometimes live. Other companies have optimized their websites, so it's now possible to play back previous episodes of their shows through the iPad.

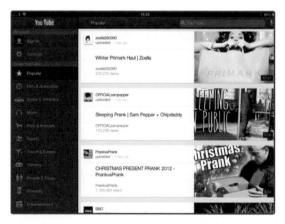

Above: YouTube is a popular video sharing site, which can be accessed through a dedicated iPad app.

STREAMING MEDIA/VIDEO

Most videos are streamed to your iPad via your internet connection, so you can start watching within a few minutes, rather than wait for it to download completely.

Above: Stream programmes from BBC iPlayer to start watching them within minutes.

- **Streaming**: with streaming, just a small amount of data is downloaded to the iPad. This is a buffer against any interruption caused by any slowdown or delay on the internet connection that could affect your viewing.

- **Buffering**: while the movie is being buffered, you see a circular, revolving line. If the film is regularly halting and the buffering icon appears, it is because of problems with the internet connection.

- **Bandwidth**: streaming video naturally takes up a lot of bandwidth. The higher the quality of the movie, the more bandwidth it needs. For example, Netflix has three levels – Good, which is up to 0.3 GB/hour; Better, which is up to 0.7 GB/hour; Best, which is about 1 GB/hour. However, if you're viewing the movie in high definition (HD), this shoots up to 2.3 GB/hour.

Hot Tip

If you are having problems viewing a streaming video, the first thing to do is choose a lower quality setting.

- **Viewing Problems**: in addition to how much bandwidth you have, streaming can be affected by other factors, such as the amount of other traffic, if you're sharing the connection, or interference from other wireless products.

SYNC VIDEOS

Having shot your video masterpiece or purchased the latest film release, you need to make sure it's available on the iPad in a format that will work.

iTUNES

Use iTunes to keep the videos on your computer and iPad in sync – or to share access to videos without having to transfer them first.

⊙ Once you purchase a TV show or movie from iTunes, it will automatically download to your iPad. The next time you sync your iPad with your computer, it will be moved to your iTunes library on your computer.

⊙ Through iCloud, it can also be automatically downloaded to other iOS devices that use the same iTunes account.

Step 3: Choose Videos from the iPad settings menu and enter your Apple ID and password under the Home Sharing title.

Home Sharing

Instead of transferring the movies to your iPad, you can play them from your Mac or PC over your Wi-Fi network.

1. To play videos from your iTunes library on Mac or PC to your iPad, you have to make sure they are both on the same home network.

2. Open iTunes on your computer and in the File menu choose Home Sharing and then Turn On Home Sharing. Enter your Apple ID and password and click Turn On Home Sharing.

3. Tap Settings on the iPad and choose Videos; under Home sharing enter the same Apple ID.

4. Now launch the Videos app and you'll see there's a new tab, Shared. Select a shared library; there may be several if you are sharing iTunes on different computers.

5. Tap the Library you want, select the type of video you want – Movies, TV Shows or Music Videos – and then choose the one you want to play.

CONVERT VIDEOS TO iPAD-FRIENDLY FORMAT

The iPad supports only a limited number of video formats. While movies and TV shows downloaded from the iTunes store and services such as Netflix will usually be iPad compatible, there are many that may not be, including your own home movies.

Convert Using iTunes

You can use iTunes to convert video into an iPad-friendly format. Add the video to iTunes by going to File, Add to Library and selecting the video file. Once you have imported it, select the video and in the File menu select Create New Version and then Create iPad or Apple TV version.

Above: You can download the Video Converter app for iPad.

Convert Using Third-party Apps

There are many third-party applications – free and paid for – that will make conversion quick and easy. Some, like Wondershare's Video Converter Ultimate, will optimize your video for playback on the iPad and, once the conversion is done, automatically add it to your iTunes library for syncing with the iPad.

Hot Tip

You may have to be patient if you use iTunes to convert your home movie. The results are not always great and, depending on how long your movie is, conversion can take a long time.

READING

iBOOKS

Through this free reader, you can read books on the iPad, whether they're downloaded from iBookstore, Apple's online bookshop, or elsewhere on the internet.

BUILDING UP YOUR BOOK COLLECTION

With thousands of free and paid-for books in iBookstore, there's plenty of choice available.

iBookstore

The book store is accessed from within the iBooks app, which is one of the iPad's built-in apps.

1. Once it's installed, tap iBooks. When it opens for the first time, you'll see a set of empty 'bookshelves' ready to hold your books. Tap Featured in the bottom toolbar to browse iBookstore.

2. This opens the Books section of the iTunes store. You can scroll down the page to see suggested titles or tap Top Charts to find out which are the most popular. The store also has Audiobook versions of many titles. Just click the Audiobooks tab to find them.

Above: Use the Categories button to browse the books in a particular genre.

3. To filter the list of available titles, tap the All Categories button at the top of the page and select which genre you are most interested in, such as Crime & Thrillers, Food & Drink, etc.

4. If you know what you're looking for use the Search box. You can also tap the Top Authors button and search by author's name, choosing between paid-for works and free.

5. Tap the book cover and the information box opens with all the details to help you decide if it's one you want to read. As well as the standard book information about the publisher, author, price and so on, there is a Sample button, which lets you read a short extract from the book.

6. Below this is a more detailed description of the book, ratings and reviews by other iBookstore users and links to related titles.

DOWNLOAD BOOKS

Whether it's through iBookstore or the web, there is a variety of ways you can build up your personal library on your iPad.

From the iBookstore

1. Choice made, tap the price or Free button, then Get Book. You may be prompted to confirm your purchase or enter your password for your Apple ID.

2. A circular progress bar shows the title being downloaded and it will then appear on the top shelf.

3. Once the book is downloaded, tap the cover to open it and start reading (*see page 135*).

Internet

iBooks supports two of the most popular ebook formats, EPUB (electronic publication) and PDF (portable document format). You can find books in these formats all over the web; for example, from Project Gutenberg (www.gutenberg.org), epubBooks (www.epubbooks.com) or ManyBooks.net.

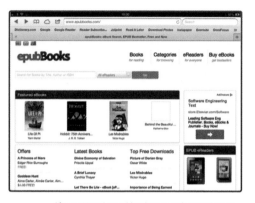

Above: Visit the epubbooks.com website to browse titles and download them to iBooks.

Step 1: Once downloaded you can choose to open your new book in iBooks.

1. To download these books directly to iBooks, open Safari and go to the site. Select the book you want, choose one of the two formats above (if available) and tap the Download link. On sites such as ManyBooks.net you can then choose to Open in 'iBooks'.

2. Similarly, if you receive an ebook or link to one in your email, tap it and it will be added to iBooks.

3. Alternatively, if you have already downloaded the ebooks to your computer, you can transfer them to iBooks on your iPad, via iTunes. Just drag the EPUB book file into your iTunes library on the computer (or select Add to Library from the File menu in iTunes and choose the file). When you sync your iPad with the computer, the ebook will be transferred to one of the shelves in iBooks.

There is a third format that iBooks supports – interactive textbooks, where the text includes images, sounds, videos, animations and even 3D objects. These are made using a special Apple format and are available only in the iBookstore.

Automatic Downloading via iCloud

All the books you buy from iBookstore will appear in your iBooks library but are actually stored in iCloud, Apple's online storage and backup service. This means that if you purchased a book on your computer or iPhone, you can download and read it on your iPad.

- **Purchased**: If it's a book you've already purchased, tap the Purchased icon at the bottom of the iBookstore screen. Tap the Cloud icon beside the book you want to download.

- **Sync Books**: In order to automatically sync books purchased across all your iDevices, tap Settings, then iTunes & App Stores and turn on Books in the Automatic Downloads section.

ORGANIZING YOUR BOOKS BETWEEN DEVICES

You can choose to have all your books organized in the same way on all of your iOS devices, like ipad and iPhone. To do so go to Settings, iBooks and turn on Sync Collections. If you'd prefer to manage your books separately between your iOS devices follow the same procedure and set Sync Collections to off.

Above: You can remove the virtual bookshelves to display your books in a more traditional list view.

Remove the Shelves

While the virtual bookshelves appeal to some, others find them irritating. For a more traditional list view, tap the button with three white lines on the right of the toolbar.

Rearrange Your Books

- **In Bookshelf View**: Tap the Edit button, and then touch and hold the book until it zooms out, and place it in a new position.

- **In List View**: Tap the Edit button in the top-right corner and then drag the book, using the grabber handles, to a new position in the list.

Hot Tip

You can also sort books in list view using the buttons at the top, so that they are displayed by title, author or category.

Delete Books

- ○ **To delete a book**: Tap the Select button and choose one or more books. A white tick will appear on each one chosen. Tap the Delete button to remove the books, then Done.

- ○ **In List View**: You can also delete a book by swiping your finger from right to left and tapping the Delete button that appears.

Book Collections

If you've got a series of books on a particular subject, group them into a collection.

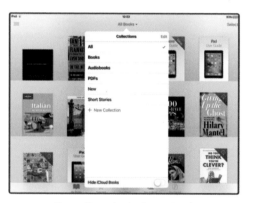

Above: All new downloads are assigned to a pre-set collection, but you can also create a New collection.

Hot Tip
You can save PDFs direct to iBooks from your email, Safari or other apps. When you view the page or document click the Share button and select Save PDF to iBooks.

- ○ **Pre-set Collections**: iBooks comes with three pre-set collections: Books, Audiobooks and PDFs.

- ○ **Libraries**: Collections are shown in separate libraries. To switch between them, tap the button showing the title of the current Collection and select the one you want.

- ○ **New Collection**: To add your own group of books, tap Collections, and then New, and write in a name. Go to the collections that currently house the books. Tap the Select button, choose the titles you want in the new collection and press the Move button. Select the new collection and the ebooks will be moved there.

- ○ **Delete a Collection**: To delete a collection, tap the Collections button, select the one you want from the list, tap the Select button and press Delete. Deleting a collection also removes all the books in it.

READERS

The lightness of the iPad, and the iPad mini in particular, gives it a natural advantage for reading books – especially when it can also hold most of your library.

eBOOK READERS

Most ebook readers work in a similar way. Apple iBooks, shown below, allows you to bookmark pages and write notes, and will remember where you last finished reading.

Reading on the iPad

1. Open iBooks and tap the cover of the book you want to read. If you have already started reading a book, iBooks will automatically open at the last page you read.

2. Generally, if you hold the iPad in portrait view, there'll be one page to a screen. In landscape view there will be two pages.

3. To turn a page, tap the screen on the right and flick left. To turn the page back, tap the left of the screen and flick to the right.

4. As you read, there's nothing on the page to distract your attention. To access the Reading controls at the top of the page and the Page Navigator at the bottom, touch the middle of the page. To close them, touch the page again.

Step 4: When you read on an iPad there are no reading controls which may distract you. To access them, touch the middle of the page.

Navigating the Book

- **Library button**: Takes you back to the bookshelf or list view of your books.

- **Contents button**: Tap this to jump to the Contents section. Scroll through the list of what's in the book and tap any of the headings to go direct to that page. Tap the button, now labelled Resume, to return to where you were.

- **Move to a page**: Drag the slider at the bottom of the page. As you move across, there's a text box with the Chapter heading and page numbers. When you let go, the book will open at that page. Alternatively, tap the magnifying glass icon and type the page number in the box.

- **Revisit a page**: Use the Go to Page XX link or Back to Page XX link at the bottom of the screen.

Hot Tip

You can also turn a page by tapping the left or right margin. To activate this feature tap Settings, iBooks and turn on Both Margins Advance.

Above: Navigate through your iBooks by touching the screen to show control icons such as bookmarks, contents, and the slider at the bottom of the page.

Bookmarks

If there's a particularly notable passage in the book that you know you'll want to revisit, bookmark it. Tap the bookmark icon in the far right corner. You can access all your bookmarks at any time by tapping the Contents icon and selecting Bookmarks.

Notes

Highlight a key passage or add a note by tapping-and-holding any word. Use the endpoints to choose the exact content you want. Then use the pop-up menu to do the following.

○ **Copy**: Then paste into a document – handy if you want to add a reference to an essay or review.

○ **Define**: Learn the word's meaning and how it's used.

○ **Highlight**: This opens several other options, including a choice of highlight colour, adding a note or switching to underlining.

○ **Note**: This opens the same yellow note box you can choose in the highlighting options. Add your comments using the on-screen keyboard. You can access all your notes by tapping the Contents button and selecting Notes. To delete a note, remove all the text in it.

Above: Tap and hold to select a word or phrase, and choose from options to define, highlight and so on.

○ **Search**: Lets you find where the same word or phrase is used, which is particularly useful in non-fiction books for searching for all references to a key topic.

○ **Share**: For licensing reasons, this feature is not available everywhere. Where it is tap some highlighted text, then the Sharing button. It opens with options to add the highlighted quote to an email, text message, Tweet, Facebook update and more.

Changing Appearance

In iBooks you can adjust the text and layout of your ebook to make it more comfortable for reading. Tap the letter A icon.

○ **Screen brightness**: use the slider to adjust.

○ **Font size**: Tap the smaller letter A to reduce the size of the text and the larger one to increase it.

Hot Tip

Back up your bookmarks/notes, so you don't lose them and can also access them on any other iDevice you use. Tap Settings, iBooks and turn on Sync Bookmarks.

Above: Tap the AA button to improve readability by adjusting font choice and size.

○ **Fonts:** Choose the font that offers the best readability.

○ **Themes:** Change the background colour. Remove the virtual book imagery and read the book as one continuous page by turning on Scrolling View.

○ **Justified text:** If you find it easier to read a book in which the text is evenly spaced across the line, go to Settings, iBooks and switch on Full Justification.

Searching Text

Tap the magnifying glass icon at the top of the page and type in the word or phrase you are looking for. All references to it that are found are displayed in the text box below. To widen your search to look on the Web or in Wikipedia, the online encyclopedia to which anyone can contribute, tap the relevant button.

Read Aloud

Save your energy when reading stories aloud and have the iPad narrate the tale for you. iBooks can read stories aloud using the VoiceOver screen reader that aids accessibility to the iPad for visually impaired users.

Read Aloud

1.   To find a Read aloud storybook, tap Featured in iBooks and then type Read aloud in the Search bar.

2.   Tap the chosen book to open it and then the loudspeaker icon on the top menu. Under Read aloud select pages to turn Automatically and then tap Start Reading.

3. The storyteller starts and the text is highlighted word by word.

4. To move to any page, use the scrub bar at the bottom, which has tiny thumbnails showing where you are in the book. (If it's not visible, tap the middle of the page.) Slide your finger along the bar to the place you want and tap the word you want to start from, and the story will continue from there.

5. To pause reading at any point, tap the loudspeaker icon again and then Stop Reading.

Above: After downloading a read aloud book tap the loudspeaker icon on the top menu. You can then select pages to turn automatically and tap Start Reading.

OTHER BOOKSTORES

There are several rival online bookstores, such as Google Play Books and Amazon's Kindle Store, for which you'll need different apps.

Hot Tip

With Read aloud editions of books, words are highlighted as they are spoken by the narrator, which is a real boon for youngsters learning to read.

Google Play

This is Google's alternative to the iTunes store. Primarily aimed at those who use Android devices (which rival Apple's iOS devices), its books can be read on the iPad through the Google Play Books app, available from the App Store.

Google claim their bookstore has the world's largest selection of ebooks, including millions of free titles, but because of Apple's policies you can't shop for new titles direct from the app. Instead, you have to access the store through Safari (or your iPad or your computer) and purchase the titles you want online. They will then automatically appear in the Google Play Books app, so you can read them. The book controls are similar to those in iBooks and you can download the books for reading offline, when you have no internet connection.

Kindle

Kindle for iPad is the free reading app from the Amazon bookstore. There are more than one million free and paid-for Kindle books available. As with Google Play Books, you have to get your titles online. Amazon's whispersync technology can then sync the book with any computers and iDevices that have the Kindle app. To save space on your iPad, you can store the bulk of your books in the Amazon cloud, only downloading the books that you want to read on the iPad.

As with iBooks, you can create Collections, which group your books into related areas of interest. Once you start reading the book, the last page read, bookmarks, notes and highlights will also all be synced, so wherever you are reading, you'll be able to start just where you left off.

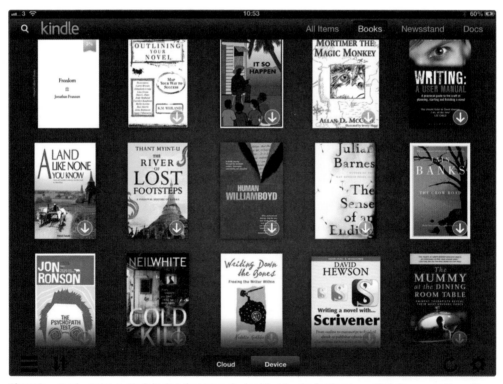

Above: Save space by storing your Kindle books in the Amazon cloud and then downloading them to your iPad when you want to read them.

NEWS

No more drying out the paper that's got wet, or reading across a page that's torn or wrinkled: the iPad is the perfect paper boy.

NEWSPAPER SUBSCRIPTIONS

The iPad offers the flexibility to subscribe to your favourite newspaper or buy one-off editions covering momentous events; several publishers refresh news content throughout the day.

Newsstand Subscriptions

Originally, most newspaper iPad editions were standalone apps. Then newspaper and magazine publishers started adding their titles to Newsstand, as it enables them to auto-renew subscriptions. That has now been replaced by the News app in iOS 9. For more details on using News, *see page 146.*

Above: Subscribing to the Mail Online allows you to update content and stay up-to-date.

Standalone Subscriptions

For publishers, the benefit of having a separate app for the newspaper is that it gives more freedom over pricing and content. Some offer a fixed version of their printed newspaper while others have standalone apps for the iPad that are linked to their website. There are various in-app subscriptions available with the benefit that you can update the content as often as you like, so you always have the latest news.

Tablet-only Newspaper

The *Daily* was the first newspaper created solely for the iPad and other tablets. As such, it took advantage of the iPad's dazzling display to present news, entertainment and sport in a striking way.

However, the pioneering venture was not financially sustainable in the long run, although it is likely to open the way for more digital-only news publications, like *Newsweek* – with premium content specifically designed for the iPad.

Create Your Own Newspaper

If you prefer to be your own editor, try Early Edition 2. Redesigned to take advantage of the Retina screen, it is a news reader that dynamically lays out the content in a newspaper format.

As with any newspaper, stories are positioned according to the importance of their content. You can also pre-load images when you have Wi-Fi coverage, so you can carry on reading your newspaper offline, when you have no connection, such as on a flight.

Above: Download the Dilbert Mobile app to access the cartoons archive collection.

Cartoons

There are celebrated newspaper cartoons available – without the newspapers. Dilbert Mobile is free (as in no charge) when downloaded from the App Store and even gives you access to the 20+ year archive of the entire collection of office-life humour.

> ## Hot Tip
> The best of the magazine and newspaper apps are customized to take advantage of the iPad, so will have a completely different look and feel from the newspaper, with unique navigation and interactive features such as video, music and live links on the page.

RSS FEEDS

Subscribe to a news site's RSS feed and you can keep up with breaking news and get regular story updates. All you need is an RSS news feed reader (also known as a news reader) for the iPad.

Above: Get personalized suggestions in your RSS feed by using one of your social network accounts to log in. Or manually add your favourite websites.

Using a News Reader

There are several news readers available in the App Store, including Feeddler, Newsify and Feedly.

Most websites today, whether it's a blog, news site, online magazine or entertainment site, will have an RSS feed. RSS stands for Really Simple Syndication and is the standard way for websites to publish the latest news and updates.

Adding a News Source

Feedly is shown here, but most readers work in a similar way.

1. Once you have downloaded and installed Feedly, tap to launch it. Tap the three line icon (known as the hamburger or menu button) at the top and then click on the Login button.

2. For your convenience you can get personalized suggestions by logging in through your Google or Facebook account. Choose how you want to login, then Feedly will open the relevant app and ask you to sign in.

3. Feedly allows you to assemble in one place content from a vast array of sources, including publications like the New York Times, most blogs on the web, YouTube channels and many

more. To find a source, copy and paste a topic or website address in the search bar in the top corner or tap the hamburger icon, and then Add Content.

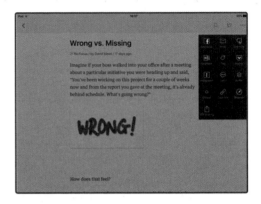

4. When the page opens tap the + sign to add the RSS feed to Feedly. The left-hand menu opens with the option to add the new feed to an existing collection of sources or create a new one. Now when you tap your source in the left-hand menu a list of stories will appear in the main pane. Tap the headline, and the full article will be loaded.

Above: Once you've opened the story press the More button for different share options.

5. Press the More button (three dots) and you have a number of options for sharing the story, opening the associated webpage or saving it to read later.

Mix in Your Social Life

Described as a Social News Magazine, Flipboard allows you to mix in your news feeds from Google Reader, newspapers (such as the *Guardian* and *New York Times*), blogs and the like with information from your Facebook newsfeed, Twitter timeline, YouTube videos, Instagram photos and other social media.

As a result, you have a personalized magazine where your news and that of your friends, is scattered among national and international news, plus other feeds that match your interests.

> ### Hot Tip
> A news feed – RSS feed – includes a summary of new articles, links, and details of when they were published. The feed is read by news reader software, which can pull in feeds from thousands of sources.

Create Your Personalized Magazine

1. Go to the App Store and search for Flipboard. Press the Free button, and then Install App, and when it has finished downloading, tap to launch.

2. The front cover shows the main featured Flipboard stories, like any magazine, but unlike any printed issue, you can tap the refresh button to change the stories.

3. Tap the Flipboard Account button to login or sign up. This allows you to personalize your magazine, save stories for later and access them from any device.

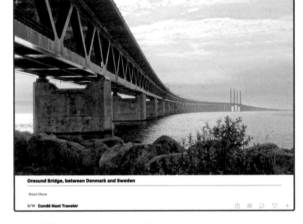

4. The tiles show different sources from which to create your personal Flipboard. Tap any tile to see more. Once in a section tap the story to see the original article and pictures.

Oresund Bridge, between Denmark and Sweden

Read More

8/10 Condé Nast Traveler

Step 4: When you open a story on Flipboard you can choose to add a comment or tweet it.

5. Along the bottom are various icons for sharing the story – adding a comment, retweeting it, marking it as a favourite or posting it online to read it later.

6. Tap the three line menu button to see which sites and social networks currently make up your Flipboard. You can add more social networks from the list or search through the different categories that interest you to see more potential sources. You can also search by keyword to find more sources that might interest you.

7. When you find a source you want to add to your board, tap the + button to add it to your Flipboard.

MAGAZINES

**No more need to be weighed down with a pile of glossy magazines.
Carry the contents of several magazine racks with ease on your iPad.**

NEWS

Get the richness and vibrancy of your favourite magazines and newspapers, wherever you are,
on the high-resolution iPad screen.

Getting the Publications

News is Apple's replacement for newsstand, which put all your magazine and newspaper
subscriptions in one place. Rather than whole publications, News collects stories together from
the sources you choose, based on topics you want. There are five main sections in the app.

- **For You**: These are the stories from the channels and topics you follow. The more you
  read, the more these stories will be personalized to your tastes.

Above: The News app creates a personalized
collection of stories for you to read.

- **Favourites**: These are the channels and topics you
  follow. To add a new one tap the + sign when
  viewing a channel or topic. To remove one, tap Edit
  in the top corner and tap the X mark on the channel
  or topic you want to delete

- **Explore**: Browse suggested channels – like
  HuffPost, Sky News or techradar – or topics
  ranging from movie actors to video games.
  When you find something you like tap the +
  sign to add it to your Favourites.

- **Search:** If you're looking for something specific type in the search bar. Tap on the result you want to go to that item.

- **Saved:** This is where your Saved stories are kept. To save a story tap the bookmark icon in the article. Swipe left to delete a saved article. To delete the History of articles you've read, tap the History tab then the Clear History button.

News versus Newsstand

Confusingly, if you used Newsstand with iOS 8 you will still have it when you upgrade to iOS 9. It will be a folder containing your existing magazine and newspaper apps as before. However, the icon for any new publcations you subscribe to will be added to the Home screen not to Newsstand. However currently News is only available in a limited number of regions.

Subscribing to Publications

You can still subscribe to most newspapers and magazines through their own standalone apps. Many of the apps are free to download with the possibility to purchase in-app an individual issue or a subscription. Any purchases are made through your Apple ID account and if you subscribe, each new issue will be automatically downloaded over your Wi-Fi connection for you to read.

Turn Off Auto-renew for Subscriptions

When you subscribe to a magazine or newspaper, it is made clear that this will auto-renew. It puts the onus on you to remember to cancel your subscription if you no longer want it, before it's due for renewal. Although it's not made clear, you can cancel auto-renewal at any time.

> ## Hot Tip
> To save your data allowance, you might not want to download new editions for all publications automatically. Go to Settings, News and turn off Mobile Data.

Above: To delete the History of stories you've read in the News app tap Clear History.

1. Tap Settings, then iTunes & App Store.

2. Tap your Apple ID and in the box that opens select View Apple ID. You may be asked to enter your password.

3. Scroll down and tap Manage App Subscriptions (if you don't have any, this button won't show). Choose the subscription from the page that opens and turn Auto-Renewal to Off, then tap Turn Off in the confirmation box that opens.

DIGITAL MAGAZINE VIEWER

Rather than reinvent a publication for the iPad, some publishers prefer to make the digital version as close to the original print copy as possible.

Zinio

○ **Digital editions**: With Zinio you get an exact copy of the print edition in digital format, plus, sometimes, extra content in the form of video and audio.

○ **Digital publisher**: Claiming to be the world's largest newsstand, Zinio is the digital publisher for hundreds of magazines around the world.

○ **Download the app**: You can then explore a series of free sample articles, which you can also share on Twitter, Facebook or LinkedIn.

○ **Browse through different categories**: Browse to find the

Above: The Zinio app features exact copies of print magazine edition in digital format, as illustrated by this article from a film comment magazine.

magazines you want. They are usually available to purchase as a single issue or on subscription.

- **Standard format**: The magazines are turned into a standard format, so they can be read through the Zinio reader, which is available for desktop computers, as well as for the iPad.

Above: Download the Comics app to buy and read comic books from major publishers.

COMICS

With its great display and reputation as the Superhero of the Tablets, the iPad is a natural medium for reading comics and comic books.

Comic Readers

- **Many comic apps**: There are many apps to choose from that enable you to access some of the great classic comics – from the Beano to Marvel Comics and the X Men or DC Comics and Superman.

- **Free to download**: Like newspapers and magazines, the apps are free to download but there are in-app charges for purchasing a single issue of a comic or a longer-term subscription.

- **Comics**: Instead of downloading the apps separately, you can use apps like Comics, which are digital readers that let you buy and read comics and comic books from many of the major publishers. They publish many of the digital comics the same day as the print edition is published, so you don't miss out. You can search for titles according to popularity, genre, publisher and even creators. There are also free comics for you to try.

ENTERTAINMENT

ENTERTAINMENT MACHINE

The iPad is as good a music player as any, with the advantage of a bigger screen to browse through your collection. But you'll need three apps – iTunes, Podcasts and Music – to get all the features you can access in iTunes on your computer.

Hot Tip

You can play your music through the built-in speaker, attach headphones, use wireless headphones or play through your TV using AirPlay.

Above: Apple Music app has been given a redesign in iOS 10. A new 'For You' tab has news of your favourite artists and recommends songs you might like.

USING THE MUSIC APP

This is the place to play all your audio content, whether it's music and audiobooks from iTunes, taken from your CDs or streamed from one of the internet music services.

Play Music

By default, Music is one of the main buttons in the Dock that's accessible at the bottom of every Home screen.

1. Tap the Music icon to open it. In the splash screen that opens you'll have the choice to Join Apple Music, Apple's streaming service or, as here, Go to My Music.

2. You'll see your music, with Recently Added songs at the top and a list of Artists underneath. Select the tile of the song you want and then press the Play button to start the song. Tap again to pause.

3. Just above the toolbar, the red line (playhead) moves to the right along the scrubber bar to show how far you are through the song. Tap here and the music controls go full screen, making it easier to move the playhead backward and forward, to go to a different part of the song.

Above: The iPad music player displays the controls, scrubber bar and volume slider at the top.

4. Above the progress bar you'll see an image featuring the song title and artist. At the bottom tap the Repeat button (two arrows in a loop) to play the song again. Beside it is the Shuffle button (two arrowed lines meeting and separating) which plays the songs in a playlist in a random order.

5. Tap the Back button or the Forward button to move to the previous or next song. If the song is playing, tapping the Back button just returns to the start of the track.

6. To alter the volume, use the slider at the top or the physical buttons at the side of the iPad.

Up Next

When you start playing a song in the Music app, a queue of songs that will follow is created. This is called Up Next.

1. You can see what's coming by tapping the Up Next button (an icon of three lines). Here you can add or clear songs from the queue by tapping the right link.

2. The app chooses what music to add to the Up Next list according to the track you're playing. If you randomly picked a song from your library, the Up Next feature will also pick random songs from

Above: The Up Next list shows what songs will follow. To change the order of the songs click the three line icon on the right of one of the tracks.

My Music. If the original track is from an album, the queue will consist of other songs from the album, or if it's a track by an artist who has several songs in your library, the list will feature other tracks by the same artist.

3. If you're listening to Beats 1 or Apple Music radio the Up Next list will be blank.

Let Siri Be DJ

On the iPad 3 and later, take the stress out of changing track and let Siri control your music. Start by tapping-and-holding the Home button.

> **Hot Tip**
>
> **To display the music controls quickly when you're in another app, swipe up from the bottom of the screen to open the Control Center.**

- **Play music**: say 'play music' or 'play'; 'pause' or 'stop' to halt the music; 'next song' or 'previous song' to change track.

- **Play a series of songs**: dictate 'Play album <name>', 'Play artist <name>' or 'Play playlist <name>' and all songs under that name are played.

- **Shuffle current playlist**: by saying 'Shuffle' while it's playing.

- **Get track information**: ask 'What's playing?' or 'Who sings this song?'

FIND YOUR MOOD MUSIC

The music you feel like listening to at any particular time will change. To make it easier to find the sound that suits your mood, try Apple's streaming music service.

Apple Music

For a monthly subscription you have access to over 30 million songs, plus unlimited radio, personalized and curated music lists, hand-selected by experts as well as your own music library.

It should mean you're never stuck for the right music to suit the occasion and if you ever are, Apple has plenty of pre-made playlists to inspire you. It's a fantastic way to have all kinds of new and old music at your disposal. Tap For You to join up.

Search Songs

Rather than scroll through one long list, you can locate a particular song you want by tapping the magnifying glass icon and typing in the Search box. Select the appropriate tab to search Apple Music or your library.

ADDING MUSIC

You can add music directly to your iPad through the iTunes app or sync music gathered from other sources (as long as it isn't copy protected), through your computer.

iTunes App

Access the online music store to download music directly to your iPad.

1. Tap the app to go online to the iTunes store and select Music at the bottom.

2. If there's a particular type of music you like – from Pop to Hip-Hop – select it using the Genres button at the top of the screen.

3. Scroll down the page and you can see lots of different selections, such as new albums, themed collections, what's hot and what the Apple staff are listening to. There are also recommendations just for you. If you know what you want, use the Search box at the top.

Above: Apple Music is a streaming service that puts hand-selected music, radio and your library, all in one place.

4. Once you have selected an album or song, tap to go through to the information page. This includes details of the artist, the release date and average rating by other iTunes users, plus the price button. Underneath is a listing of the track(s).

5. Tap the song title to listen to a 90-second sample of the track.

6. To buy an individual track, tap the price button to the right and then the Buy button. If it's the album on which the track features that you want to buy, tap the price button at the top of the page.

7. If you have a big collection, you may end up trying to buy a track you have already purchased. If this was bought in the iTunes store, Download appears instead of the price, so you won't be charged again.

Step 6: Buy a track by tapping the price button to its right, and then the buy button. To buy the whole album, tap the price button at the top of the page.

8. While the items are being downloaded, tap the More button and then Downloads to see their progress.

Other Music Sources

○ **Amazon MP3 Store:** Amazon's online music store was the first to offer song downloads that were not digitally rights managed – that is, DRM-free – so they could be played on virtually any music player relatively easily. Today, they still have a huge selection of music and offer consistently low prices.

○ **Subscription music sites:** For a regular monthly fee, services like Spotify and Apple Music allow you to stream music to your iPad as well as download it to play offline.

- **Your music collection**: add your favourite tracks from your CDs or downloaded MP3 files.

- **Musician sites**: like Bandcamp – which lets musicians sell their music (as downloads) direct to fans.

PODCASTS

There are thousands of hours of podcasts – audio and video shows – on a stunning range of topics that covers virtually everything from self-help to hobbies. Time to tune in.

Above: The Bandcamp website enables musicians to sell their music downloads directly to fans.

Finding Podcasts

Previously, finding and playing a podcast involved two apps. You would first search and select a show using the iTunes app and then play the podcast from the Music app. Now Apple's free Podcast app is all you need. When you open the app, it will show your library with any podcasts already downloaded.

1. To see all the available podcasts, tap the Featured button (the star icon at the bottom of the screen). This shows you the New and Noteworthy podcasts, as well as Editors' Choice and Featured Collections.

2. To select different genres, tap Categories at the top of the screen and scroll down to see what is available. Select Cancel and then Top Charts to see a list of the most popular podcasts.

Hot Tip

The Podcast app removes the podcasts and controls from the Music app. This means it's not possible to create playlists that include podcasts. Similarly, Audiobooks are now found in iBooks, when previously they were in the Music app.

3. Tap any that interest you, and the information box gives you full details of the available episodes, how long they are, together with other users' ratings and reviews.

4. Tap on the title of a single episode to preview or stream just that one. It will start playing.

5. Press the Subscribe button, and the latest episode will be downloaded. You will also get future episodes downloaded automatically as they become available.

6. Press My Podcasts and you'll see all episodes that are already downloaded from podcasts you have subscribed to. Tap Unplayed at the bottom to see any podcasts which you have not yet listened to.

Browse the Popular Podcasts

1. Tap Top Charts at the bottom of the screen. This shows the most popular podcasts in different categories.

Above: Browse the Podcast store by category and tap any that interest you to find out more information and download.

Hot Tip

You can choose which pocast episodes to download to your iPad. Go to My Podcasts, select the podcast you're subscribed to and tap the gear icon. Select Download Episodes and you can choose whether only new or unplayed episodes are downloaded automatically or none at all. On this page you can also choose to keep or delete episodes you have listened to.

2. Tap Categories for a dropdown list of all those available. To explore the category you are in, swipe up or down.

3. Tap the podcast icon to see details about the individual episodes, as well as a general description, reviews and related podcasts.

Play Your Podcasts

In My Podcasts you can view your podcasts as a series of tiles (icons) while Unplayed shows a list of the podcasts you've not listened to organized by date. There are two ways to play your podcasts:

Step 2: Browse popular podcasts within a category by swiping up or down.

- ⊘ **Streaming**: tap any episode and it will start playing wihtout being fully downloaded first. To do this, you should be connected to Wi-Fi.

Hot Tip

You can organize your podcasts into stations that update automatically on all devices. Tap My Podcasts, then the + sign and tap Add Station. Name your station, tap Save and add your preferred podcasts.

- ⊘ **Download**: tap the More button (three dots) next to any episode of a podcast you're subscribed to and select Download Episode. Now it will be stored on your iPad and you can listen to it even when you don't have a Wi-Fi connection. Once it's downloaded tap the podcast and it will start playing.

Control Playback

When you begin playback, the podcast controls appear in a bar towards the bottom of the screen. Tap the bar to view the controls full-screen.

Above: Starting Podcast playback displays the controls in a bar at the bottom of the screen.

Audio Playback Controls

○ **1x button**: lets you change the playback speed: 1x is normal, 1/2X plays at half speed, while 2x plays at double speed.

○ **Replay button**: with the number 15 inside a left-pointing loop: tap this to go back 15 seconds in the podcast.

○ **Play/Pause button**: toggle this to start playing the podcast or pause it.

○ **Skip Forward button**: with the number 15 inside a right-pointing loop – this moves the podcast forward 15 seconds.

○ **Up Next button**: shows what episode is set to play next. This is normally the next episode of the podcast.

○ **Volume slider**: move left or right to set the volume.

○ **Playhead**: tap, hold and drag this to move to another part of the podcast. Move your finger to the top as you drag left and right and you can skip backwards and forwards more accurately.

○ **Share button**: The box with an arrow coming out opens the Share box so you can send a link to the podcast by mail or text or you can post it as an update to Twitter and Facebook and the like.

Above: Tap the playback bar and the controls will appear in full screen view.

○ **Sleep timer**: this is handy if you want to be lulled to sleep by music or someone reading a story. Choose how long you want the podcast to play before it stops.

Video Playback Controls

There are similar buttons to control viewing of your video podcast. To access them, simply tap the screen while watching the video.

Delete Podcasts

In My Podcasts swipe to the left over the chosen podcast and press the Delete button. If you just want to delete unplayed episodes tap Unplayed, then Edit. Select individual episodes then tap delete. To delete stations go to My Podcasts, tap edit above the station list and then tap the red dot.

SYNCING MUSIC

While the iPad is a great entertainment centre, it doesn't have as much space as your computer for holding all your songs, etc. So when it comes to syncing with iTunes, it pays to be selective.

iTunes Sync

Connect the iPad to iTunes on your computer and it will appear in the top bar.

1. Click Music in the sidebar. If you're using iCloud Music Library to hold all your music in one place you don't need to sync your music with iTunes. If you don't you can choose to Sync Music with your Entire Music Library. However, as you are likely to have more music than will fit on your iPad, the safer option is Selected playlists, artists, albums and genres.

2. You can also choose to add music videos – although be careful if you have a lot, as these tend to be very large files and will quickly eat up your free space – and voice memos.

3. Now go through your playlists and select those you want on your iPad.

Above: When using iTunes to sync music from your laptop to your iPad, select the option to sync Selected playlists, artists, albums and genres. You can then go through these different categories and tick those which you would like to copy over to your iPad.

4. Do the same for artists, albums and genres. Don't worry about duplication. Even if you choose an artist whose songs are on the playlists or genres you've also selected, only one copy of the actual song will be copied over – although you'll still see it referenced in each list.

5. An alternative option is to create your own special playlist that has all the songs you want to copy over to your iPad. Then select only this playlist to sync.

6. Click Apply to sync your changes now.

iTunes Match

Subscribe to this service for an annual fee and you can sync your music collection using Apple's iCloud. All your music, including music from CDs or other online stores, will sync with Apple's servers rather than iTunes on your personal computer. You will see your entire music collection on your iPad but it will be stored on iCloud.

ORGANIZING YOUR MUSIC

The bigger your music collection the more difficult it is to keep under control. Fortunately, playlists make it easy to organize your sounds to suit your mood, while features like Home Sharing and music streaming make it possible to listen to your music without overloading your iPad.

MUSIC SETTINGS

When it comes to playing your music, there are several features you can change to suit your personal preferences. Tap the Settings icon, then Music, to get started.

Changing Sound Levels

○ **Sound Check**: turn this on to play all songs at roughly the same volume, even if an individual track is louder or softer.

○ **Equalization (EQ)**: changes the quality of the sound to suit the type of music you are listening to. There are 23 different effects, ranging from Bass reducer to Spoken word. Generally, these settings apply only to music played through the Music app, except for Late Night. This setting applies to video as well. As it reduces volume in loud parts and increases it in quiet sections, it's particularly good for listening to music in a noisy place, such as on an aeroplane.

Above: Choose from Equalization effects to adjust sound settings to suit certain types of music.

○ **Set a Volume Limit**: for when the children have grabbed the iPad to play their music. Tap Volume Limit, and then adjust the volume slider.

PLAYLISTS

These are mini-collections – lists – of songs based on a theme, which can be as personal or as general as you wish. For example, you could have a playlist of the songs played at your wedding, all 1990s songs in your Library or your Adele collection.

Create Playlists: Step-by-step

Playlists that you create on your iPad can be synced with iTunes on your PC or Mac.

1. Tap the Music app to open and then the Playlists button. There you'll see any existing playlists. To start a new one, tap the Create a Playlist button.

2. In the box that opens give the play list a name that readily describes its content.

3. Tap the Add Songs button beside and select those you want to add to the playlist or click the Add All Songs button.

4. You can select songs by Artist's name, album title, genres and so on.

5. The list of Songs on your iPad opens. Tap the + button beside those you want to add to the playlist.

6. When you have added all the songs you would like to your playlist, just tap the Done button.

Step 2: Enter a name for your new playlist.

Step 3: Tap the Add songs button to start selecting music by Artists, Albums etc., that you want to include on your playlist.

7. Your new playlist will be copied to the iTunes library on your computer next time you sync your iPad.

Edit Playlists

Rather than create a new playlist, you can change an existing one.

1. Tap Playlists, select the playlist to modify and press the Edit button.

2. Tap Add songs to add more tracks to the playlist in exactly the same way as creating a playlist above.

3. To delete a song, tap the red button and then press the Delete button that appears on the right-hand side.

4. Tracks in the playlist are played in the order in which they appear. To change the song order, tap the Drag handle on the right and move it up or down.

5. To delete a playlist altogether, press the Playlists button, tap and open the playlist then tap the More button and select Delete.

Step 6: Sync your iPad to copy your new playlist to the iTunes library on your computer.

Hot Tip

Once you've set the volume limit, stop someone else changing it back. Tap Settings, General, then Enable Restrictions. Enter a four figure Restrictions Passcode and re-enter it for security. Under Allow Changes, select Volume Limit, and then tap Don't Allow Changes.

Radio

There are various ways you can explore different types of music and get expert, personal recommendations. In Music tap the Radio button and you can access Beats 1. Always On, it features top DJs and curated playlists that let you explore new music in a variety of genres. You can also create your own custom stations based around your pick of artist or song.

Step 5: From the Genius playlist you can add to Up Next or a different playlist.

Hot Tip

You can follow the artists in your Music library. To do so search for an artist then tap Follow. Go to Connect and you can view the content that they share.

Step 6: The Genius Playlist shows up in your All Playlists, marked by the atom icon.

Creating a Genius Playlist

1. Based on the type of music and artists you like, Music will suggest other songs you might enjoy and create a genius playlist. If you don't see it you need to turn it on. Go to Settings, tap Music and then toggle Genius to on. Tap to agree to the terms and conditions.

2. Play the song on your iPad for which you want related recommendations, then tap the More button (three dots) and then tap Create Genius Playlist.

3. You need to have enough similar sounding music for Genius to create its list. If you do, the new Genius playlist appears, named after the song it's based on. Tap it to play the suggested songs.

4. If you're not keen on the recommendations, tap the Refresh icon at the top to get a new list.

5. Tap the More button at the top and you can add to Up Next list, add to another playlist or download the track to listen offline.

6. Press playlists and you'll see your Genius playlist is there, marked by the special icon of an atom.

Deleting Songs

To delete a song from the iPad, press the More button (three dots) next to the song, then tap Delete in the pop-up box. This will remove the song from your iPad, but it will remain in your iTunes library on your Mac or PC, or on iCloud.

HOME SHARING

Play music on your iPad from the iTunes library on your computer – without having to download the music files.

Setting up Home Sharing

For Home Sharing to work, your iPad and computer must be on the same Wi-Fi network.

1. Open iTunes on your Mac or PC, go to the File Menu, Home Sharing and choose Turn On Home Sharing.

Step 6 Tap Artists to see the Home sharing option.

2. You'll be prompted for your Apple ID and password. Enter these and then click Create Home Share.

3. On the iPad go to Settings, Music and under Home Sharing enter the same Apple ID and password.

4. Open the Music app and tap My Music, then select Artists to open the dropdown menu. Near the bottom you'll see Home Sharing.

5. Tap that and you'll have the option to see the music on your iPad or in the library stored on the computer. Choose this option and you can see and play the music from your computer.

STREAMING MUSIC

Instead of storing and playing your own music, you can get songs, radio shows, concerts and more streamed, on demand, to your iPad.

Streaming Music Apps

As well as Apple Music, there are several other on-demand music services that allow you take your pick from millions of songs and discover new artists.

○ Typically, these services offer the wide spectrum of music – from rock, pop and funk to the classics. Some include talk radio, covering sport and comedy.

○ While several sites offer a free service with upgrade to **premium** paid features, such as removal of ads or listening offline, you usually have to pay a **monthly subscription** to get the most benefit from the iPad app.

○ Among the services with iPad specific apps are **Spotify** (spotify.com) and **TuneIn Radio** (tunein.com) both of which have extension apps for the Apple Watch. **Slacker Radio** (slacker.com) is only currently available in the US.

Above: Spotify has an iPad specific app.

○ There are also many other on-demand music services to choose from in the App Store that allow you to stream music. **Last.fm**, for example, doesn't have a specific iPad app but does have iPhone versions that will run on your tablet.

○ As Last.fm is a music recommendation service, the app tracks the music you and you friends have been playing and gives music recommendations based on that. It can be a good way to discover new music.

Concerts

Get the best of the bands – from Coldplay to The Who – playing for you on your iPad. Qello streams HD concert film to your tablet. Subscribe and you get unlimited access to their concerts and can create your own set lists.

Airplay

For great sounds around the home, you can use Airplay to play music from your iPad through your Hi-Fi speakers, wherever they are.

Above: Use Airplay to play music from your iPad through Airplay capable devices with Hi-Fi speakers, such as Apple TV.

All you need are AirPlay-enabled speakers, which are available from well-known manufacturers like Denon, B&W, JBL and so on in the Apple Store.

As well as the music, all the information about it, such as the song title, artist's name, playing time and so on, are also streamed across your Wi-Fi network.

Using AirPlay

1. The quickest way to access AirPlay is to swipe up from the bottom of the screen. In the Control Center you'll see the AirPlay symbol. Tap this to open the options box. You'll see the iPad and any other AirPlay-capable devices, such as Apple TV, on your home network.

2. Select the receiver you want to use and a tick appears beside it. In Music, tap a song and it will start to play through the device you selected.

3. Control the sound from your iPad, using Music's audio controls to play or pause a song, skip a track or change the volume.

4. To return playback to the iPad, tap the Airplay icon again and select iPad from the list.

Stream to Your Computer

If you don't have AirPlay-enabled speakers, you can still get a bigger sound for your music (and see video on a bigger screen) by streaming it from your iPad to your Mac or PC. You will need some extra software

Above: AirServer app allows iPad-to-computer streaming.

to enable this iPad-to-computer streaming. AirServer (www.airserverapp.com) is inexpensive and available for both the Mac (used here) and PC.

Setting up Streaming

1. Download and install AirServer to your computer. You will need to activate it by entering your email address or activation code supplied when you purchased the software.

2. The AirPlay logo is now available in the computer's menu. Click and select Preferences then Advanced and Automatically Launch on Startup, so that the service is always running.

3. Also in Preferences select Audio, and you can choose which speakers you want to use – typically, this will be System Default. Click Remote Volume Controls Output Device to use the iPad as your remote control.

4. To connect your iPad to the computer, swipe up from the bottom of the iPad screen to open the Control Center and tap the AirPlay button. You'll see a list of AirPlay-enabled devices. Among them will be the computer on which you installed AirServer.

5. In the options box select your computer, then tap your song and it will start playing through your Mac or PC.

STORING MUSIC

Despite the limited space on the iPad, it's possible to have access to your music any time, anywhere by using online storage services.

iTUNES MATCH

With iTunes Match you can access your entire music collection, even songs imported from CDs or bought online, from your iPad.

Music Match-maker

iTunes Match is a paid subscription service that lets you store your music library in iCloud – that is on Apple's servers – rather than your own computer. It means you can access and play your music from your iPad virtually wherever you are.

Getting Started

You can sign up for iTunes Match on your computer. Open iTunes, go to Store menu and select iTunes Match. Below the brief overview of iTunes Match click the button to subscribe and enter your details. Your subscription is tied to your Apple ID.

Above: Use iTunes to activate iTunes Match. You will be asked to enter your Apple ID.

Matching Tracks

Once you're subscribed, iTunes Match looks through your music library, matching any tracks you have against the 26 million plus songs in the iTunes store. These are added to your music library in iCloud. The matched tracks play back at high quality – 256-KBps AAC DRM-free – regardless of the quality of your original track.

Hot Tip

You can store up to 100,000 songs in iCloud, big enough for most music collections.

Step 5: Download tracks for offline listening by tapping the iCloud symbol.

Step 8: You can turn off automatic renewal of iTunes Match in Settings, iTunes & App Store.

Any songs that can't be matched are uploaded to iCloud. How long this will take depends on the number of songs and the speed of your connection.

Listen to Your Matched Music

1. iTunes will scan, match and upload any unmatched tunes. A status indicator lets you track progress.

2. iTunes Match will overwrite any existing music or playlists on your iPad, with full details of your iCloud library.

3. The download icon – of a cloud with downward-pointing arrow – is shown next to items available for download from iCloud. If it's not shown if the item is already in your local iTunes library.

4. Tap the song title and it will be streamed from iCloud, via your Wi-Fi connection, and downloaded fully as it plays.

5. Tap the cloud to download tracks so you can play them when you don't have an internet connection.

6. Once you play a track on a playlist, playback continues automatically down the list, whether the song is already downloaded or is still in iCloud.

7. The iCloud status of individual songs shows if it was purchased from iTunes, added from Apple

Music or matched with iTunes Match. Go to
iTunes on your computer, click my Music,
then Songs in the right-hand corner. In the
same menu, click Show Columns, then iCloud
Status. Matched, shows songs matched
with iTunes Match.

Hot Tip

**Song files larger than 200MB or
longer than two hours in length
won't be uploaded to iCloud.**

8. By default iTunes Match will automatically renew the annual subscription. To change it,
   choose Settings on the iPad, then iTunes & App Store, sign in if necessary and tap View
   Apple ID. Scroll down to iTunes in the Cloud section and turn off iTunes Match renewal.

iTunes Match vs iTunes in iCloud

iTunes Matching is a paid-for song-matching and storage service. iTunes in iCloud is a free
service which means that anything you've bought from the iTunes store, such as music, can be
automatically downloaded to your iPad. While iTunes Match tracks are downloaded DRM-free,
Apple Music files downloaded for offline listening are digitally rights managed (DRM). So unless
you keep a backup of your DRM-free tracks you might not be able to play your music without
an Apple Music subscription.

Other Cloud Services

There are several other online services that will
let you store and play your music – either
streaming it from the cloud or downloading to
play on your iPad. Amazon Music with Prime
Music app lets subscribers stream over a million
songs, download them to play offline and access
songs in their collection that they have bought
from Amazon. Google Play Music is another
option. It provides free, ad-supported radio in
the US.

Above: The Amazon Music with Prime Music app also lets
you play songs from the cloud.

MAKE YOUR OWN MUSIC

Several popstars, including Justin Bieber and Adele, have been discovered after recording their songs at home and posting them online. Try for yourself, using the iPad to make your own music.

TUNE UP YOUR LIFE

Whether you are a professional musician or have no musical knowledge at all, GarageBand for iPad will get you hitting the right notes.

GarageBand

Apple's GarageBand is a fantastically sophisticated program, which lets you record backing tracks for your songs, videos or just your amusement. There are three types of instruments used to record sounds.

- **Smart instruments:** great if you have no musical know-how. They cover guitars, keyboards, bass and drums and ensure all the notes and chords you play are in tune with each other.

Above: You can use GarageBand's touch keyboard to play and record songs.

- **Touch instruments:** best if you play guitar, bass, keyboards or drums for real. Tap the virtual instruments on screen to create your sound, but beware: they are pressure sensitive. The harder you press, the greater the volume of the piano note or sound of the drum.

- **Real instruments:** give the most authentic sound. You'll need to connect your guitar, keyboard or drum pads to the iPad directly. For example, you can connect a USB keyboard to the USB port using Apple's Camera Connection Kit.

RECORD YOUR SONG

GarageBand for the iPad is a paid-for app available from the App Store. Download and install, then tap to open.

1. Choose your instrument. Swipe left or right to see what's available. In this example, the keyboard is selected.

2. The keyboard opens. Tap the image of the Grand Piano and select the type of keyboard, from Electric Piano to Classic Rock Organ.

3. If you don't like the keyboard layout, press the keyboard button on the right and you have two rows of keys for left and right hands.

4. Tap the keys to play your notes. The spot where you tap and the force of your tap dictate the precise sound and volume.

Step 2: Tap the Grand Piano image and select a keyboard type, such as Electric Piano.

5. Tap the button in the middle to change how the keyboard moves when you swipe it. Glissando is more like a piano, whereas swiping plays the notes smoothly. Switch to scroll and swiping moves you left or right on the keyboard.

6. When you're ready to record, tap the red Record button in the top bar. The metronome starts and counts through one measure before recording begins and the Play button turns blue. Tap this to stop recording.

7. If you fluff the notes, tap the Undo button and start again. Press the View button to change to Tracks view, where you can see the music you recorded. Tap once to select it and press the Play button to listen to it.

Step 8: Tap the loop icon and drag a clip from the list onto the mixing deck.

8. To add to your song, tap the loop icon and drag a pre-recorded clip from the list onto the mixing deck. Tap Instruments and select other sounds to record, like drum, guitar or bass.

9. To save your song, tap My Songs in the control bar.

Build a Song

To create a song in GarageBand, you record the Touch instruments and then arrange the recordings in Tracks view. You can have up to eight tracks.

1. Select Tracks view in the top control bar. You'll see each row is a track, which has the recording of one Touch instrument, shown as a rectangular block. The icon beside the recording shows which instrument it is.

2. Swipe this icon to the right to reveal the track controls where you can control the relative volume of the track within the song.

3. Move blocks of music around by tapping-and-dragging them to new positions in the song. To trim the clip, push the edges in.

Hot Tip
Double-tap on a track – or region as it's called – and you get the editing controls: Cut, Copy, Delete, Loop and Split.

Sharing a Song

Once you're happy with your song, there are several ways to share it. Tap My Songs, then the Select button. Select the one you want, and then tap the Share button in the top-left.

You'll see there are options to share the song on social media, such as Facebook or YouTube, email it or save it as a ringtone.

GAMES

When it comes gameplay, the iPad's large screen gives it a natural advantage over its smaller screen rivals, particularly if you have a Retina display to display the high-quality graphics.

STANDALONE GAMES

Whether you're a casual or serious gamer there's plenty to keep you entertained with apps specially made to take advantage of the iPad's increasing processing power.

Games Store

Download games direct to the iPad from the App Store. Simply tap the App Store icon to open and select Categories from the top bar. In the box that opens you can select Games then choose from All Games or the genre that interests you most. As you will see, there are games that cover the whole spectrum from action and adventure to board games, racing, strategy and puzzles.

Popular Games

There are thousands of games available in the App Store, so it's good to get personal recommendations. To see what others are playing, select the App Store, tap Categories then All Games and Top Charts at the bottom.

Hot Tip

Playing with touchscreen controls takes a little getting used to compared with physical controllers, so it might be as well to practise before challenging friends.

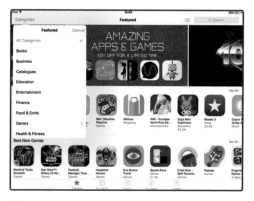

Above: Download games from the App Store by selecting Categories in the top bar and choosing the type of game you are looking for.

Here you can see the most popular free and paid-for games, as well as those that have grossed the most money. If there's a particular type of game you're looking for, such as Arcade or Kids, tap the All Categories button in the top-left, select Games and make your choice.

Below are five of the most addictive games that also show why the iPad is great for gaming.

- **Angry Birds Star Wars**: who wouldn't be angry when you're blasted through space. Amazingly popular and compulsive to play, Angry Birds are now the rebels having to battle Darth Vader in a Star Wars adventure. If you get tired with that fantasy, don't forget there's Angry Birds Space, Rio, Seasons and so on.

- **The Dark Knight Rises**: most blockbuster films now have a tie-in game to build on their popularity. This one gives you the chance to be Batman and fight your way, with the help of some useful gadgets, through the dark streets of Gotham City.

Above: Angry Birds is one of the most popular games in the App Store. There are many different versions to try.

- **Tiger Woods PGA Tour**: experience life as a golf pro, stand on some of the world's best fairways, check out your swing and see how you stack up against the real pros. You can also earn rewards by completing challenges across other golf games.

- **Scrabble**: the traditional word game has had a makeover and comes with exclusive features for the iPad. There are HD Graphics to take advantage of the iPad screen, sound effects and animations plus up-to-date dictionaries to help put a stop to the arguments about what words are allowed.

- **Farmville 2 Country Escape**: Farmville is often described as the world's most popular farming game. This free game lets you go on farming adventures to collect rare goods and craft new recipes as well as managing the ploughing, growing and havesting on your farm. Raise animals and grow your farm with help from your friends. Join a farm Co-Op to trade and share or play on your own in Anonymous Mode. You can also play the game when not connected to the internet.

Above: The Game Center app lets you play games against other people and shows leaderboards of scores.

SOCIAL GAMING NETWORK

Test your gaming skills against your friends – or strangers around the world – using Apple's multiplayer gaming app, Game Center.

Getting Started with Game Center

Game Center works on the premise that gaming is more fun when done socially. Game Center itself is a built-in app that lets you play games against other people, see what apps are available and get some bragging rights (or not) by showing a leaderboard of best scores on a game.

1. Open the Game Center app by tapping its icon, and then enter your Apple ID and password to sign in. If you want a separate Apple ID for gaming, tap Create New Account instead.

2. Even if you are signed in through your existing Apple ID, you can change the details that show in the Game Center.

4. Tap Settings then Game Center. If you see an option to sign in you can change your Apple ID now. If not, tap your existing Apple ID then Sign Out. You can now enter a new Apple ID and password and sign in.

5. Tap your Game Center Profile. Under Privacy, tap to switch off Public Profile if you want only your friends to see your profile and don't want to be recommended to play with other gamers you don't know. If you are happy for everyone to see your details, turn this on. Tap Done when finished.

Playing a Game

Tap the Games button at the bottom of the screen. You can go with any of the recommendations there or, to buy a particular game you want, tap the Search bar and enter the details.

Scroll through the free and paid-for games for the iPad that have been developed to run in Game Center. Tap the one you're interested in and press the price button (or Get if it's free) and then tap Install App Download.

Once it's downloaded, tap the Game's icon and you'll see the game's leaderboard. Tap the Play Game banner. Depending on the game, you can access the Game Center by tapping the Game Center icon on screen or pressing the Home button and then selecting Game Center from the Home screen.

Above: Choose a game from the suggested recommendations or tap Search to look for a specific game.

Playing with Friends

1. When you're ready to try out your skills against some competition, tap Friends, choose one, select the game and tap Play.

2. If no friends are listed, send a request. Tap Friends on the bottom bar and select them from the left-hand panel. To add them from your Contacts list, tap the + button.

3. If more than two players can play the game together, select additional players to invite to the game and tap Next. Send your invitation and wait for the reply.

4. If none comes, or your friend isn't available, tap AutoMatch and Game Center will find someone to play. Alternatively, you can tap Invite Friend to try someone else you know.

Above: To play games against friends, send out requests by tapping Friends and tapping the Send Friend Request button. You can also add friends from your contacts by tapping +.

5. Once everyone is ready, you can start the game.

6. If a friend invites you to play a paid-for game you haven't got, you will have to purchase it. To do so, tap Friends, then their name. Tap the game you want, then tap the price at the top of the screen.

Hot Tip
Once you have achieved some impressive scores, you can challenge people to try to beat you. Tap the score or achievement you are proud of and then tap Challenges.

LIFESTYLE

Whether it's an essential life skill, such as cooking, or life enhancing, such as a Vogue Cropped T-Shirt, it will be covered in one of the thousands of lifestyle apps available for the iPad.

SHOPPING

The high street has gone online. Most major retailers have an online store accessible using Safari on the iPad. Many have also developed their own tablet apps, from department stores such as Debenhams to fashion stores (H&M), home furnishing (Ikea) and food delivery services such as Ocado. That's not forgetting the original online retailers Amazon and eBay, which are still prime destinations for iPad shoppers.

There's also a new breed of online store, such as Fancy, with dedicated apps for the iPad. Fancy is part social network, shopping catalogue and wish list. Ideas are crowd-sourced, recommended by savvy users, but unlike other collector sites such as Pinterest, the majority of items are also for sale.

Above: The Fancy iPad app allows you to share your wish lists and purchases with other users.

FOOD AND DRINK

Foodies in need of a recipe can try Epicurious, which also creates shopping lists based on the dish you choose. If you can cook only with expert advice from celebrity chefs, try Gordon Ramsey Cook with Me HD or Jamie's Recipes from Jamie Oliver. To wash it all down, mix your own Speakeasy Cocktails.

SPORTS

The sporting life is covered, with everything from the Everyday Golf Coach HD, analysing your swing, to ESPN ScoreCenter for iPad, covering results and news from sports around the world.

HEALTH AND FITNESS

Got a spare moment? Do some exercise with Fitness HD or Pocket Yoga HD. Go too far and you may need a medical self-help app to aid the diagnosis, but it must be remembered that an app should never replace medical advice from a health professional.

TRAVEL

Wherever you're planning your trip, there's an app to help. TripAdvisor lets you check out hotels, flights and restaurants in your planned destination with reviews and ratings by other users. If you prefer to travel in spirit rather than the flesh, fly around the planet from your iPad with Google Earth, explore different cultures and distant lands with the digital app version of National Geographic Magazine or explore the universe with NASA App HD.

Above: There are many weather apps which can be adjusted to your location.

REFERENCE

Previously, when there was a lively discussion in the pub or elsewhere, it was difficult, if not impossible, to prove who was right. Now it takes a moment's research on the iPad. What causes a plane's vapour trail? Look it up in Wikipedia, through one of the companion apps like Wikipanion. Get the low-down on the high-life of Al Capone in Encyclopaedia Britannica or test your romantic streak with a look at the sonnets in the app that covers the complete works of Shakespeare. More mundanely, what are the prospects of rain for the school sports day? Check it out with one of the myriad of weather apps that can be customized to your locale.

WORKING

NOTES

One of the key ways of staying organized is to jot down a note when something occurs to you. With the Notes app you can sync with other iDevices and your computer, so you're always on top of what you have to do.

Above: The note that is currently open is highlighted in yellow in the left-hand pane.

Hot Tip

A list of accounts and notes are shown in landscape mode. To see just the note tap the double arrow icon or turn the iPad to portrait view.

TAKE NOTES

Notes isn't designed for writing your novel or essay, as it doesn't have the rich formatting features of programs such as Word, but is perfect for writing notes.

Add a Note

Tap the Notes icon of a ruled writing pad on your Home screen. Notes will automatically open the last note that you wrote. If this is the first time you've used Notes, you can just tap the screen where you want to type, and the keyboard appears. To start a new note, tap the pen and paper icon in the top-right corner.

Navigating Notes

It is easy to navigate your notes.

1. In portrait mode, tap the Notes button and a pop-up window lists all your Notes accounts.

2. Tap the account you want and the notes are listed with the date they were written or updated, from the most recent to the oldest.

3. The note that's currently open is highlighted in yellow. Simply tap the note you want, and it opens in the main window.

4. When the iPad is in landscape mode, the list of accounts and their notes is permanently shown.

5. To search the text of your Notes scroll to the top of a list of notes to reveal the Search box, then type in the word or phrase you are looking for.

6. You can also search for a specific attachment by selecting the four squares icon in the lower-left corner.

Delete Notes

Tap the dustbin icon at the top of the screen to remove a note. In list view swipe left or right across the note title and then tap the Delete button.

Hot Tip

The title of your note is the first line of text, which means you can end up with some pretty odd headings. It's a good idea to put the title you want as the first line of text.

SYNCING NOTES

So you can always be up-to-date with your jottings, you can sync notes between your iPad, your PC and other iDevices, as well as share them directly with others.

Sync with iCloud

Use iCloud to keep any notes made in the Notes app on the iPad in sync with your computer and other devices, such as the iPhone and iPod Touch.

If you're using an Apple email address with iCloud (such as yourname@me.com or yourname@mac.com), tap Settings then iCloud and switch Notes to On.

Above: If you have an Apple email address you can sync your Notes through iCloud by toggling Notes to On in the iCloud settings menu.

Above: When you create a note using Siri it will be attached to an email address. You can change this address through Settings, Notes.

Alternatively, if you're using Gmail or a similar email account with iCloud, then go to Settings, select Mail, Contacts, Calendars and turn on Notes for the account.

Share Notes

While reading the note, tap the Share button at the top of the screen. You can then choose to email the note, send it as a message or print it, using AirPrint.

Notes Accounts

When you create a note, it is attached to a specific account. You can have several different accounts in Notes.

- **Email accounts:** as well as an account for notes created On My iPad, there may be others. Typically, these are attached to email accounts. In many email readers you may see a notes folder that contain these messages. There is usually an option to display the notes or not.

- **Different accounts:** all of these can be accessed in Notes itself, by tapping the Accounts button (in portrait mode you may have to tap the Notes button first).

- **Specific accounts**: to see only the notes in a specific account, choose that account from the list. If you then tap the + button, it will create a new note in that account.

- **Default**: to choose which account to use as the default for new notes, go to Settings, tap Notes and make your choice.

- **On your iPad only**: go to Settings, then Notes and toggle on the On My iPad switch and your notes in this account appear only on your iPad.

SKETCH A NOTE

Notes doesn't just present a typed list of what you have to do. You can also sketch an idea or plan on iPad 4, iPad Air and later, iPad Pro series, iPad Mini 2 and later.

Finger Art

1. To get started tap the squiggle icon and use your finger to sketch, then tap Done. Tap the sketch in your Note to edit it.

1. Tap your preferred choice of sketch tool on the left – including pencil, marker or pen tool.

2. To see more colours swipe the colour palette left or right.

Above: Draw your idea or plans using your finger and the sketch tools in Notes.

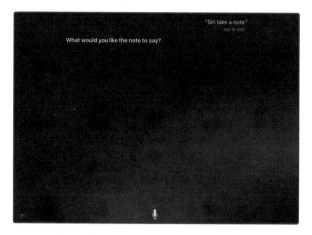

"Siri take a note"
tap to edit

What would you like the note to say?

Above: Summon Siri, request 'Take a Note' and start dictating.

3. Tap the ruler tool for it to appear in the note to make it easier to draw a straight line.

4. If you want to close in on the details, pinch open your fingers to zoom in or pinch closed to zoom back out. Drag two fingers lets you move the sketch around.

5. Start again, if you are unhappy with the results by touching and holding the eraser tool, then selecting Erase All.

DICTATE YOUR NOTES

As a virtual personal assistant, Siri is just what you need when it comes to finding, dictating and updating your notes. Unfortunately, he only works with an iPad 3 or later.

Find a Note

Summon Siri by tapping-and-holding the Home button. Ask to 'Show all my notes' or notes with the keyword you are looking for, such as 'Show my note about birthday presents.' Tap the note in Siri's list and it opens in the Notes app.

Dictate Your Note

Get right to the point and tell Siri to 'Take a note' and then dictate your message.

Update a Note

If it's some time since you wrote the original note you'll first have to find it. Tell Siri, 'Update Note' and select the one you want from the list. Alternatively, give sufficient detail to help Siri find it, such as 'Update note on February sales forecasts' and then dictate the additional text. Tap on the microphone when finished.

DOCUMENTS

The iPad lets you create, view and edit documents just as if you were at your desktop computer, and has built-in sharing and syncing too.

CREATE DOCS

While a touch screen keyboard may not be as practical as the one on your computer for creating long or complex documents, it is still possible to produce some great-looking work.

Writing on iPad

Given that it is a mobile app, Pages is an amazingly powerful word processor. It is available as a free download from the App Store.

Creating a Document

1. Once downloaded, tap Pages to open it. On the Documents screen tap the + button in the top-left corner. If you already have documents created in Pages on your Mac or elsewhere, there are options to connect via iTunes, a web browser or your iCloud Drive.

2. Tap More and there are other locations available, including cloud storage sites like Dropbox and OneDrive. If you are starting from scratch, tap Create a Document.

Above: Pages allows you to choose a template from existing formats, or create your own by selecting the Blank option.

3. Choose a Template from the selection, which includes pre-formatted documents, such as posters, party invites, plus different letter and report styles. To create your own, select Blank.

4. When you open a template, it will include dummy text. To edit this and replace it with your own, double-tap the screen, and the keyboard will appear.

Above: When editing a document you can change the preset template text by highlighting the passage you want to change. Use the keyboard to enter your own text and the options at the top of the keyboard to adjust settings such as font size and alignment.

Editing a Document

⊙ **Change the text**: highlight the part you want to alter and use the settings at the top of the keyboard to change the font, font size etc.

⊙ **Edit styles**: for paragraphs and headings, etc. select the text and tap the Paintbrush icon in the top bar. Tap the Layout tab and you can change the number of Columns and Line Spacing.

⊙ **Add Photos, Tables, Charts or Shapes**: just tap the + button in the top-right and make your choice.

⊙ **Resize a graphic**: tap it and push one of the blue anchor points to amend.

⊙ **Settings**: press the spanner in the top-right corner and Document Setup to alter paper size, margins and so on.

Working with iWork

Pages is part of the iWork suite of programs, which also includes Numbers for spreadsheets and Keynote for presentations. There is now a single format for the apps on iOS and the Mac that enables Handoff. So you can stop working on Pages on the iPad and pick up where you were on the Mac and all the latest edits will be there.

If you have iCloud set up on your iPad, the three iWork apps will automatically back up your documents to your iCloud Drive on Apple's servers. The changes are then synced to your Mac and iDevices, so any alterations made to your documents on the go are immediately available when you're back in the office.

Sharing iWork Files

While iCloud makes it simple to move your iWork documents between your Mac or PC and different iDevices, there are other ways to share your files.

Sharing Documents

When the document is open in Pages, Numbers or Keynote, tap the tools button – with the spanner icon – at the top, then select Print.

- **Print**: sends the document to any available network AirPrint printers (see page 32 for more on printing).

- **Document setup**: lets you choose which areas you want to print.

Above: Share your documents by selecting from the options in the Share box.

Tap the Share button and you can choose to:

- **Share Link via iCloud**: this makes it easy to collaborate with colleagues or family on a document.

- **Open in Another App**: first select the format to save it in, then choose from the list of available apps that can open it.

Dealing with Numbers

Numbers for iPad lets you access, create and edit your spreadsheets on the go. Even if you're sent a spreadsheet that wasn't created with Numbers, you can work on it, as the program can open Excel documents or spreadsheets saved as comma-separated value (.csv) files. This can be extremely helpful.

Getting Started with Numbers

Open Numbers and you have a choice of templates, from expense reports to a loan comparison, savings sheet or invoice. To set up your own, select Blank. Choose one to get started and tap to open.

○ **Edit text**: to change the text in a cell, double-tap, then tap to select the text entry box that appears and type in your changes. The Text icon (T) on the keyboard should also be selected.

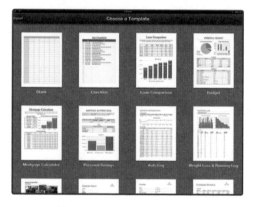

Above: Numbers provides you with a variety of template options to use as the basis for your document by entering your own data and words.

○ **Edit numbers**: double-tap the cell where you want to change the figures and select the Numbers icon (42) to open the calculator.

○ **Equations**: for more complicated spreadsheets. Tap the = icon on the keyboard and you have access to a calculator with a wide range of functions, from the financial to the statistical.

○ **Date and time**: can be added by selecting the clock icon from the keyboard, accessed by double-tapping a cell.

Change Styles

To alter the appearance of your spreadsheet, tap a cell and then press the paintbrush icon on the top bar. Choose the relevant tab to alter:

- **Table Styles**: select the Table tab and choose the layout you prefer or set them manually by tapping Table Options.

- **Headers**: extend the size of header rows and columns and add a footer if required.

- **Cell**: tap Text Options to change the font, size and colour. Use the other buttons to alter alignment and the Border Style or the Fill Colour of the cell.

- **Format**: you can change the cell format so that, instead of a number, it contains a percentage, date, text or checkbox, etc.

Above: Cell text options allows you to adjust font characteristics and styles so that any headings or labels appear as you would like them to.

Creating Presentations

Could business life survive without the presentation? Certainly not at the moment, so if a presentation is needed quickly or there are some last minute changes to your slides, Keynote on the iPad is your answer.

- **Start a New Presentation**: open Keynote and then tap Create Presentation. To get started, choose one of the stylish templates available as your theme for the slides.

- **Edit the Presentation**: the theme is a single page at the moment. To add more, tap the + icon in the bottom-left. To edit the current slide, just double-tap on the text and type in your changes using the keyboard that appears or press the microphone and dictate to Siri (iPad 3 and later).

Hot Tip

The easiest way to see changes in your data is to add a chart. Tap the + button on the Numbers toolbar, select the Charts tab and choose the type of chart to add. Tap the blue box to select the cells on which the chart is based.

○ **Change Styles**: tap the paintbrush icon and you can change font sizes and styles, the appearance of lists and the layout.

○ **Resizing Images**: double-tap the picture and use the blue anchor points to adjust the size. Tap the paintbrush icon on the toolbar and you can style the borders and flip the image.

○ **Build Your Presentation**: press the spanner icon and you can change the way the slides build up and the transitions between them. You can also add Presenter Notes and print your presentation. To share them tap the Share button.

Above: When using Keynote for presentations you can change styles by tapping the paintbrush icon and selecting from the options displayed.

Blogging on iPad

Often the best ideas for your blog come as you browse the web. Blogsy for iPad takes advantage of this by having its own built-in browser, which makes it easy to drag-and-drop images and web links right into your blog post.

Likewise, you can add photos and videos from your iPad or photo albums on sites such as Facebook and Flickr with just a swipe of the finger. As it supports most blogging platforms, including Wordpress, Blogger, Tumblr and TypePad, it should work well with your personal and professional blogs.

Drawing on iPad

Celebrated British artist David Hockney pays testament to the brilliance of the iPad as a drawing tool. He has used the Brushes app to create more than 400 works, first on the iPhone and then on the iPad. Several of the works were displayed, on the iPad, naturally, at the

Above: You can use the iPad as a very effective drawing tool, as demonstrated by the successful series of works produced by David Hockney using the brushes app.

exhibition Me Draw on iPad in Denmark's Louisiana Museum of Modern Art.

EDIT DOCS

As many businesses use Microsoft Office for their word processing, spreadsheets and presentations, there are apps that let you work with these on your iPad.

Office on the Move

Microsoft now provide separate apps that are part of their Office Suite for managing your business documents. Among them are Word, which lets you view, create and edit word processor documents, Excel for spreadsheets and PowerPoint for presentations. These apps also work with your Apple iWork files, Google Docs and other online file storage services.

Getting Your Office Files

You can sync your Office apps through Microsoft's OneDrive cloud service storage so any changes you make to the files are automatically updated. You can also open documents sent as email attachments in Word, Excel or PowerPoint.

Google Docs

Rather than keep your files on one computer, online storage services let you access your files and in some cases edit them from anywhere you have internet access. Among the most popular services for business is Google Docs. With this free service, the documents you create are stored on Google Drive.

Above: Use the Google Drive app to access and organize documents stored on Google Drive.

1. Use the Google Drive app, available from the App Store, to access your documents.

2. Tap the document to open it and then Google will open it in Google Docs to edit. If you don't have it, you'll be prompted to download it.

3. To share your document in Google Drive, tap the More button (three vertical dots) and click Add people. You can now add the names of those you want to invite to edit, comment or view it.

Hot Tip
If the file sharing section isn't visible it means that you don't have an app that can share files through iTunes. It will appear once you do.

SYNC DOCS

While some apps let you sync your business documents with iCloud and other online storage services, the majority use iTunes to transfer files between your PC or Mac and the iPad.

File Sharing

1. Open iTunes on your computer and click the iPad icon on the top menu bar, then Apps.

2. Scroll down the page to the File Sharing section and choose the app from the list on the left that has the files you want to transfer.

3. On the right it will show all the documents on the iPad. Select one and click the Save To button to select where to save the file on the computer.

4. To transfer a file from your computer, click the Add button and browse to where it is located then click Open.

PRINT DOCUMENTS

While we increasingly view documents on a screen of some size, there are times when we do need to print out a hard copy.

AirPrint

AirPrint is Apple technology that's built into the iPad's operating system, so you can print directly to a printer. Unfortunately, it's not quite that simple. The printer itself has to be AirPrint-enabled and on the same wireless network as your iPad.

Hot Tip

There's a growing list of manufacturers, available on Apple's website, who have added AirPrint support to their printers.

Above: You can install programs like Printopia on your Mac or PC and use it as a means of wirelessly printing your iPad documents.

Print through Your Computer

With this method you install a program on your Mac or PC that receives your print job from the iPad and sends it to the printers your computer uses. Printopia (www.decisivetactics.com/products/printopia) is among the programs available for this.

Print Wirelessly

Provided the printer is on the same wireless network as the iPad, there are apps that will print directly to Wi-Fi printers. Alternatively, if your printer is physically connected to your computer, by the USB port, for example, several apps have a desktop helper application for your computer, so you can wirelessly send your document to your Mac or PC to process for printing. Apps available for this include PrintCentral and Printer Pro.

CALENDAR

The hectic pace of modern life makes it more important than ever to get organized. With your iPad digital assistant you can keep up-to-date with all your calendars – at work and play.

MANAGE YOUR SCHEDULE

The Calendar is a core app that's already on your iPad. Use it to set up your events and set alerts, so you don't miss anything.

Calendar Views

Select the view you want – by day, week, month or year – by tapping the tabs at the top. Each calendar uses a different colour to mark its events, so you can see at a glance when there are busy work periods, for example.

Creating Events

1. In any view, tap the + button, and a new event box appears.

2. Enter a name and location for the event.

3. Tap the Starts section to bring up the date and time controls, and enter the details.

4. Select Repeat and choose how frequently it reoccurs, then select the calendar to add it to. When finished, tap Done.

Above: Tap the + button to add a new event to your calendar by entering the name, location, time and details.

Use Siri

Even if you're not in the Calendar app, you can get Siri to add an event or check what you've got coming up if you have iPad 3 or later.

1. Press and hold the Home button, and when Siri responds, give the event details, e.g. 'Schedule haircut 3pm next Tuesday.'

2. Siri will check to see if there's a conflicting event. If there is, he will give the details and ask if you want to proceed.

3. To see what's coming up, ask Siri: 'What appointments do I have today?' or 'What's happening on Thursday?'

Edit Events

Tap the event and then tap the Edit button. In week or month view, if you've got the wrong day, just drag the event to a new date.

Search Events

If you know there's something you've been invited to but can't remember the date, search events. Tap the Search icon on the top menu bar and then enter the keywords you're looking for – such as Jeff's presentation – in the Search box.

Setting Alerts

Adding an event to your calendar is one thing, but many of us need a reminder when it's about to happen. Alerts are set in the Add Event box.

1. Tap the Alert button and select how long before the event you want to be reminded. The options vary from a week before to the actual time of the event.

2. For events such as birthdays, you probably want an earlier alert, so you have time to get a card or present. You can set the default alert period in Settings, Mail, Contacts, Calendars. Scroll down to the Calendars section and select Default Alert Times. You can change these for timed events, birthdays and all day events.

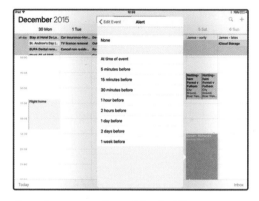

Above: You can set specific timed alerts for different events.

SHARING CALENDARS

In one calendar you can view lots of different calendars at once, including web-based calendars or even Facebook events and birthdays. You can also choose to share individual calendars with others.

Subscribing to Calendars

1. If you use an online calendar, such as Google or Yahoo!, add this by going to Settings, Mail, Contacts, Calendars, and then tapping Add Account. Select from the list or tap Other if your calendar service isn't named.

Above: You can add Facebook events and birthdays to your calendar by toggling Calendar to On in Facebook settings.

2. To add Facebook events, tap Settings, Facebook and under Allow These Apps to Use Your Account turn on Calendar (not available on iPad 1).

3. To select which calendars to view, open the Calendar app and tap the Calendars button. You'll see they are separated in the different accounts. Tap those you want visible.

Sharing Events

1. The calendar system is linked to your email. On certain email systems, such as iCloud or Microsoft Exchange, you can send and reply to meeting invitations.

2. To invite others, tap an event, and then the Edit button. Tap Invitees and select them from your Contacts by clicking the + symbol.

3. To reply to an invitation tap the invitation in the calendar. You can see who's organizing it and who else is invited, as well as who has accepted the invitation. If you add comments, only the organizer will see them.

Sharing iCloud Calendars

Instead of individual events, you can share complete calendars you have on iCloud, such as for a work project, with others. They will need an iCloud account.

Tap the Calendars button and in the section under the email address used for your iCloud account select the calendar you want to share. Under Shared with: tap Add Person and tap the + button to choose from Contacts. An invitation is emailed to them to join the calendar.

Make Your iCloud Calendar Public

You can make your iCloud calendar viewable by anyone, although they can't change anything. Follow the steps above and turn on Public Calendar. Tap Share Link and email or text the URL to anyone you want to view a read-only version of the calendar.

Hot Tip

Your colleagues will need an Apple ID and iCloud account to accept your invitation to share a calendar.

Above: You can share your iCloud calendar by adding contacts to the Shared with box, and make it public by toggling Public Calendar to On.

Sharing Other Calendars

If you want to keep a wider group, such as the office football team, organized and be sure they all know what's happening, use your iPad to set up and share a calendar on one of the free services, such as Google.

1. Open Google in your browser, click Sign in to your Google account, if you have one, or create a new one. Once logged in, select More from the main menu bar, then select Calendar. Rather than share your personal calendar, you can set up a new one. Tap the arrow beside My Calendars and select Create new calendar.

2. Fill in the details. Enter the email addresses of those you want to use it in the Share with specific people section and then tap Create Calendar.

Hot Tip

Making your project calendar on iCloud public is a good way of sharing important milestones with a project team.

Above: Use your Google account to create a new calendar and select who you want to share it with.

3. Now set up the Calendar app on the iPad. If you don't already subscribe to a Google calendar, tap Settings, then Mail, Contacts, Calendars and select Gmail. Fill in your account details and tap Save.

4. Open the Calendar app, tap the Calendars button and under your Gmail address you'll see the new calendar has a tick beside it. Now enter events, making sure that the name of the shared calendar is the one used in the Add Events box. Now those sharing your calendar will also see the event.

SYNC CALENDARS

There are several ways to make sure your calendars stay in sync but once you have chosen one, stick with it, or you'll end up seeing double.

iTunes

You can sync your calendar on the iPad with a similar app on your computer, such as Microsoft Outlook or Apple iCal, using iTunes.

1. Connect the iPad to your Mac or PC and click iPad on the top menu bar and then the Info tab. Click the Sync Calendars with box and select the type of calendar from the drop-down list.

Above: You can choose whether to sync all or some of your calendars via iTunes by clicking the relevant boxes in the drop-down list.

2. You can choose to sync all calendars or just those you select. To save space and time, you can also choose not to sync events older than a certain period of time, such as 30 days.

iCloud

By syncing via iCloud, any events you add to your calendars on your computer or iOS device can be updated on all of them, so you don't have to keep re-entering information.

1. Tap Settings, then iCloud on your iPad and turn on the button beside Calendars.

2. Go to Calendar, then tap the Calendars button and select which of the calendars listed under the Apple ID email address used for iCloud you want to sync with.

CONTACTS

Your Contacts app is far more than just a list of names and addresses; it is also your social hub from which you can send an email, text or even Tweet.

MANAGE CONTACTS

There are many ways to keep contact details of your friends, family and colleagues up-to-date.

Import Contacts

If you have your list of contacts elsewhere – in Gmail, webmail or an email program such as Outlook – then you don't want to re-enter them one-by-one. Fortunately, you can import your contacts to iCloud and sync them to your iPad.

1. As iCloud is built into the iPad, all you need to do is to activate it, using your Apple ID. Go to Settings, then iCloud, and make sure Contacts is turned on.

2. On your Mac or PC go to your existing mail program or webmail account and export all contacts in a single vCard file. How this is done will vary but the program's help file should explain what to do.

3. Still on your computer, access iCloud in your browser by going to www.icloud.com. Sign in with your Apple ID and password, then select Contacts. Click the Settings button with its gear icon that's in the bottom-left and click Import vCard.

Above: Once you have turned Contacts on in your iCloud settings the app will appear in your iCloud home screen.

4. Browse to where you saved the vCard and select it. This will import the contacts online, which will then be synced to your Contacts address book on the iPad.

Sync Contacts by iTunes

As an alternative to using iCloud, you can sync your contacts using iTunes.

1. Connect your iPad to iTunes and select it from the top menu bar, then press the Info tab.

2. Select Sync contacts and you have the choice of keeping all of them up-to-date or tapping Selected groups and checking the box beside those to sync.

3. The first time you sync with the iPad, you'll be asked if you want to merge the data, replace the contacts list on the iPad or replace the contacts on your computer with the information on the iPad.

4. You can sync contacts data from the Address Book or Microsoft Outlook on the Mac or Windows and others.

Above: Manually add contacts to your iPad by filling in the various details and tapping Done.

Add Contacts Manually

In order to add a contact directly to the iPad, tap the Contacts app to open it, then press the + button. A blank form appears. Enter the details, tapping the return key on the keyboard to move between fields.

Tap the green button beside add field, and there are options to add a contact's nickname, the phonetic pronunciation of their name, birthday, Twitter handle and so on. Tap Done when finished.

Find/Locate Contacts

As your popularity grows, so will your address book, which makes it difficult to find the contact you're looking for. Here is what to do to navigate through your contacts quickly.

- **Search**: tap the Search field and use the keyboard to start typing the name. Notice that only those names that contain the letter will appear. As you type more letters, the list narrows.

- **Tap the initial letter of the contact**: from the tabbed list on the left of the page to jump to that point in your contacts book.

- **Ask Siri**: for example, say, 'Find Thomas Smith' or if you have established your relationship with some of your contacts, ask: 'Find Mum,' for example.

Hot Tip

Don't worry about formatting, such as putting capital letters at the start of someone's name or dashes in phone numbers, as Contacts handles these automatically.

Above: Search your iPad contacts by tapping search and beginning to type the name you are looking for until it appears in the list below.

Set up Relationships for Siri in Contacts

On iPad 3 and later, Siri can use Contacts to send text messages or emails, but it is much easier if it knows who are the key people in your life.

- **Tell Siri who you are**: Siri needs to know who he's talking to. Go to Settings, General, Siri and tap My Info. Select your contact details from the pop-up window.

- **Add your relationships**: Whether it's your boss, girlfriend, mum or big brother, let Siri know the link to individual contacts by saying, for example: 'Vicky Alexandra is my daughter.' Siri will ask you to confirm the information.

- ○ **Dealing with a large family**: It could be confusing if you have several daughters, so you may have to be more specific about the relationship, such as oldest daughter or youngest daughter.

Add Relationships Manually

Tap the Contacts app to open it, select the name you want and then the Edit button. Tap on add related name field. Tap the label name to change this to the right relationship, such as brother, sister, friend, manager, assistant, partner etc., and then tap the name field to type the name or tap the information ('i') icon to select the contact from your list. Tap Done when finished.

USING CONTACTS

Once you have family, friends and colleagues set up it's easy to get in touch with them, direct from the Contacts app.

Above: Add relationships manually by going to add related name and entering the relevant details.

Sending a Message through Siri

When you have let Siri know who your key contacts are, you can simply speak your message. For example, tell Siri: 'Text my boss I'm running late for the meeting.'

Siri will locate the contact and ask you to confirm the message. If it's correct, tell Siri to 'Send.' Say, 'Change it' to alter the message or 'Cancel' to abandon it.

Off the Page

- **Save to memory**: tap-and-hold a name or phone numbe and you can copy it to memory, so it's easy to add to an email or message.

- **Send an email**: tap an email address, and it opens a new email with the address already filled in. Just add a subject line and your message.

- **Share contact**: this opens the Share box, so you can send a new message with all the information about the contact saved as a vCard. You can send the contact details via iMessages, by email, text, or to an online storage account, such as Dropbox or Evernote. If you have saved any personal information with this contact, it will also be included.

- **Send a message**: select the number to use to send a text message.

- **FaceTime**: this button shows only if you have FaceTime activated. To do this, go to Settings, FaceTime and turn it on. Tap the button, and it starts a video call.

Above: Share your contacts by sending an automatically compiled vCard.

SOCIAL MEDIA CONTACTS

On iPad 1 Twitter, and on later iPads Twitter and Facebook are built-in apps. The result is that you can add friends' Twitter handles and usernames as well as other details to their entries in Contacts.

Add Twitter

There's nothing to stop you adding Twitter details when you enter a contact's details but there is a much quicker and more certain method.

1. Go to Settings and tap Twitter. Assuming you have set up your account (*see page 79*), tap the Update Contacts button. This will compare email addresses and phone numbers from your Contacts with those used in Twitter.

2. Any matches, and Twitter usernames and profile photos will be added to individual contact details. You'll see the progress bar while it's happening, and then the number of contacts updated.

3. Tap Contacts and you'll see that several will include a Twitter username and the avatar – or profile picture – they use.

Hot Tip

Your contacts may see your Facebook email address as your preferred option. To check, go to your Facebook timeline, tap the About link and go to the Contact info section. If it's the @facebook address that's listed, tap the Edit button and change it to the address you want to use.

Above: Go to Settings, Twitter to update your contacts with their Twitter usernames and profile photos.

Tweet from Your Contacts

Tap your contact's Twitter username and you're taken to their Twitter page, showing all their latest posts and enabling you to Follow them, if you don't already. You can then tap the quill icon in the top right-hand corner to open a tweet box that's already addressed to them.

Add Facebook

Facebook works in a similar way to Twitter above. It also adds a profile photo and marks it with a small Facebook logo.

Facebook has its own messaging service and will try to use this as the default email address, rather than the one used to sign up for the service. It adds this Facebook address to the contact's details.

REMINDERS

While you can use Notes to create your to-do lists, Reminders goes a step further. Not only does it let you list your tasks and check them off, it also provides a timely alert when you have something to do.

SET UP REMINDERS

Reminders help you to organize daily life by setting up a list of all you have to do. As with Calendar events, you can set these up with dates and alarms when they have to be done or simply list them with no prompt.

Setting up Reminders – Step-by-step

1. Tap the Reminders app, which is now built in to the iPad operating system, and then tap the + sign in the top-right corner.

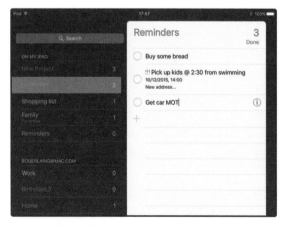

Step 2: After opening the Reminders app, you can add new reminders by tapping the + sign. Use the virtual keyboard to type your list.

2. Using the virtual keyboard that appears, type in your item 'to do', such as buy some bread or pick up kids from swimming and then tap the Return key. The titles don't need to be long, just descriptive enough to remind you what has to be done. To edit them, just tap again.

3. Add more details if you want. Tap the info button, and you can add Notes. You can also choose the priority – from high to none – as well as choose which list to add it to.

4. That's where you could leave it. Many to-do apps offer simple checklists that rely on regularly checking what to do next. Reminders goes further and will let you know when something needs doing. Tap the reminder in the list, then turn on Remind Me On a Day.

5. Tap on the date and time and use the dials to specify when you want the reminder, and then tap Done.

Create New Reminder Lists

When you create a reminder, it is added to the list in Reminders. For easier organization you can create your own 'to do' lists with more meaningful names, such as Family, Work projects and so on.

Tap Add List in the panel on the left, choose whether to add it to your iPad or iCloud account and then write in the name using the on-screen keyboard.

Repeat Reminders

Enter keywords in the Search box in the top-left, and a list of any completed and outstanding 'to-dos' appears. Tap one to select it. Tap Scheduled to see all items that are due today as well as any that are overdue.

Search Reminders

Enter keywords in the Search box in the top-left, and

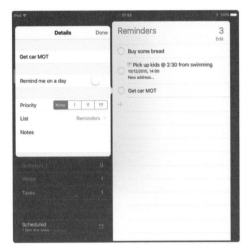

Step 3: Tap the info button to add more details to your 'to do' item in the Notes box, set its priority and choose the list to add it to.

Step 5: To set alerts for your reminders you can choose a date and time using the dials.

a list of any completed and outstanding 'to-dos' appears. Tap one to select it. Use the mini-calendar in the left-hand panel to look for all reminders due on a certain date.

DICTATE REMINDERS

If typing your to-do list is just another task you'd rather do without, get Siri to fill it in for you if you have an iPad 3 or later.

Timely Reminders

Tap-and-hold the Home button to access Siri and then say what you want to be reminded about – and when. For example, 'Remind me to book the restaurant for 7.30pm.' Before you say or tap Confirm, you can change the details by saying, 'Change the time to 8pm' or say, 'Cancel' to delete the event.

Above: Tap Scheduled and you can quickly and easily view which Reminders are due today or overdue.

Choose Your List

The reminder will be added to your default list, which is typically Reminders. To change the default, tap Settings, then Reminders and Default List. You can also tell Siri where to add your reminder. For example: 'Add butter to shopping list' or 'Add book DJ to party list.'

Hot Tip

Through iCloud you can sync Reminders, so they'll appear on your other iOS devices, such as your iPhone or iPod Touch, as well as on your Mac or PC desktop computer. Go to Settings then iCloud and turn on Reminders.

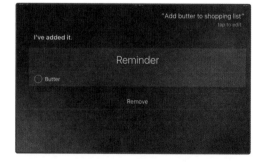

Above: You can use Siri to remind you of items on your to do list, and help with other tasks such as recording your shopping list as you dictate it aloud.

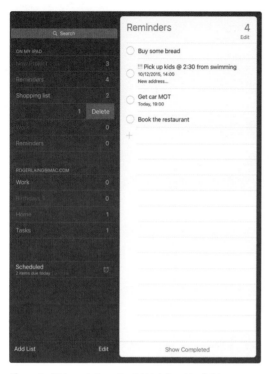

Above: To delete reminders swipe right to left and tap Delete.

COMPLETED TASKS

When a task is done, there's a tremendous sense of satisfaction from being able to mark it off as completed. Although it's finished, you can still review it. However, when your lists start to get too crowded, you'll want to remove tasks for good by deleting them.

Complete Reminders

Select a list or date from the left to view your reminders. To mark a task as completed, tap the checkbox beside it. Tap Show Completed, and you'll see, in date order, all the tasks you've finished. Hide this again by tapping Hide Completed.

Delete Reminders

Select the to-do list and you can delete individual items by swiping across the entry from right to left and tapping the red Delete button.

To delete an entire list, select it from the panel on the left, then simply tap Delete List at the bottom.

Hot Tip

If you have created a new reminder list you no longer need, tap the top-left Edit button, tap the red button beside the name of the list to remove and then press the Delete button. When you remove a list, it also deletes any remaining reminders.

ADVANCED iPAD

CUSTOMIZING YOUR iPAD

Make the iPad your own by modifying the background and changing the ways different apps and controls work.

Step 1: Select Wallpaper from the Settings menu to display icons previewing the current wallpaper.

Step 2: Tap the icons to select a new wallpaper image from the pre-supplied options or your own photo albums.

PERSONALIZING THE EXPERIENCE

Keep the pictures that mean the most to you – family, friends or landscapes – as your background, associate different sounds to individual events and set up your iPad to work the way you do.

Changing Wallpaper – Step-by-step

The wallpaper for your iPad is pasted to your Home screen and on the Lock screen.

1. In order to change it, tap Settings and then Wallpaper. The large icons under Wallpaper preview the current wallpaper.

2. Tap this and select Choose a New Wallpaper to choose an Apple-supplied image or access one of your own photos from the albums below.

3. Select the image you want and see it full view. If it's one of your own photos, you can adjust it to fit the screen. Tap and drag the image to centre on the part of the photo you want as your background.

You can also pinch to enlarge or reduce the size of the photo.

4. Tap Set Lock Screen to use it as the wallpaper there or Set Home Screen if you want it to be the background for that screen. Set both will use the same image as wallpaper on both screens.

Step 4: To set an image as your Lock Screen background tap the Set Lock Screen option.

Sounds

Make your iPad operate as noisily or quietly as you wish by turning on or off the sounds that go with different events, such as tapping on the keyboard.

1. Tap Settings and then Sounds. At the top is the slider that controls the volume on incoming FaceTime calls. When Change with Buttons is turned on, the slider also controls the Alert volume. When turned off, the volume for each is set separately.

2. Go through the list, and you can change the sound that plays with individual events; for example, the tone you hear each time you get a new voicemail, send a Tweet or trigger a Reminder Alert.

Above: Adjust options in the Sound Settings list to customize which sounds your iPad makes.

3. Turn the Lock Sounds on, and a sound plays when the Lock screen is unlocked. Similarly, switch Keyboard Clicks on if you want to hear a click each time you tap a key on the on-screen keyboard or off if you prefer not to.

Hot Tip

Rather than stick with the limited choice of Alert Tones supplied as part of the operating system, you can create your own.

Create Your Own Sounds Using iTunes

There are various apps for creating your own ringtones, which can then be synced with your iPad using iTunes. You can also create great sounds from your music collection, using iTunes on your computer. Here the ringtone's created on a PC.

1. First choose the song you want to use from your iTunes library. Right-click, select Get Info then Options.

2. In the Start time, enter the time point from where you want the ringtone to start playing. (If you're not sure where this should be, play the song in iTunes and note the time for the start point from the main bar at the top).

Above: When setting your own ringtone from your iTunes library enter time points in the Start Time and Stop Time boxes and tap OK to choose which part of the song you will hear.

3. In the Stop Time add 30 seconds to the Start Time and click the OK button. Right-click the song and select Create AAC version (once this is done, go back and uncheck the Start and Stop time, so the full version of the song plays in future)

4. Select the short version of the song in iTunes, right-click and select Show in Finder. Highlight the song title, change the file format at the end from .m4a to .m4r and confirm this in the dialogue box that opens.

Date and Time

If you're travelling, it's easy to change the time and date to match your planned destination. Go to Settings, General, then select Date & Time.

- **24-Hour Time**: turn this on if that's your preference and the iPad will display that time format (13:12 instead of 01:12 PM) in the status bar at the top of the screen.

- **Set Automatically**: turn on and the iPad will get the correct time based on your Wi-Fi or mobile connection. If you're still on your way to your final destination, you won't want this. Turn this setting off and the Set Date &Time field appears, so you can make your changes manually.

- **Time Zone**: tap this and in the Search box type the first letters of the nearest city. Select it from the list underneath, and it will automatically enter the time and date for that location.

- **Set Date and Time**: adjust these settings manually. Tap the Date and then roll the controls underneath to the correct settings. Tap Time and do the same and then tap General to return to the main screen.

Modifying the Keyboard

The more you use the iPad, the more you'll come to rely on the on-screen keyboard. Fortunately, you can get it to adapt to your way of working and add your own short cuts. Go to Settings, General and then press Keyboard.

Hot Tip

Get the time around the world with the built-in Clock app. Tap to open and select the World Clock tab. Tap any clock face to open the Search box for a city in the time zone you want. A white clock face shows it's daytime, a dark face night-time.

- **Auto-Capitalization**: automatically capitalizes those pesky first letters of a sentence or name that you may forget to do.

- **Auto-Correction**: the faster you tap, the more likely you are to make mistakes. This will automatically correct common errors.

- **Check Spelling**: always handy when you're writing an email to the boss.

- **Enable Caps Lock:** by default this is turned off. When it's turned on, you can • double tap the Shift key to activate it, so that everything you write is in capital letters.

- ".": looks strange but is very useful. By double-tapping the space bar you can automatically add a full stop and a space at the end of any sentence.

Changing Keyboards

Tap the Keyboards button to change the layout to match your language or country, whether it's for Canadian English or traditional handwritten Chinese. To swap between Keyboards, tap the Globe icon on the bottom row of keys of the on-screen keyboard.

Split Keyboard

Turn on if you want to separate the keyboard to different sides of the screen.

Hot Tip

One of the easiest ways to divide the keyboard is to tap-and-hold the keyboard key on the on-screen keyboard, and then slide your finger to Split. To return to a single keyboard, press the same key and select Dock and Merge.

Above: Split and merge your keyboard by tapping the keyboard icon and selecting Split (left) and return to single keyboard by tapping the icon and selecting Dock and Merge (right).

Short Cuts

These can save a lot of time if there are several common phrases you use in Word documents or emails. Under General, Keyboard, Text Replacement there's one shortcut already written. Type omw and On my way! appears. To add your own, such as a tagline to add to your emails, tap Edit then the + button. Write out the full phrase and then add the letters you want to use as a short cut.

SUSPENDING NOTIFICATIONS

Do Not Disturb will silence alerts and FaceTime calls for a period of time that you set. A moon icon is shown in the status bar at the top of the screen when it's active.

Turn on Do Not Disturb

This prevents notifications from lighting up your screen or making a sound – but only when your iPad is locked or sleeping. To turn it on go to Settings, then Do Not Disturb and choose the various options.

Change Your Do Not Disturb settings

Go to Notifications and tap Do Not Disturb.

○ **Scheduled**: lets you select the quiet hours, the automatic time period when Do Not Disturb operates. For example, this could be at night from 22:00 to 07:00 when you're likely to be sleeping.

○ **Allow Calls From**: this creates the exceptions to the Do Not Disturb rule and allows incoming FaceTime calls from your Favourites or selected Contacts.

Above: Customize your Do Not Disturb settings via the Settings menu.

○ **Repeated Calls**: if someone's calling you urgently, they can get through. By turning this on, the second call will ring through if the same person calls twice within three minutes.

iPAD'S OPERATING SYSTEM (iOS)

iOS is Apple's operating system for mobile devices such as the iPad, iPhone, iPod touch and, just to be different, Apple TV. iOS is regularly updated with new features.

Updating to a New Version

Each new version of iOS fixes some problems, such as security patches for Safari, as well as adding new features. Because some of these additions, such as Siri, depend on a lot of processing power they are not available on all versions of the iPad. For example, you can only upgrade the first generation iPad to run iOS 5 (currently version 5.1.1), whereas later iPads can all be upgraded to run the current version iOS 9 and later. Even so, there are some physical differences that mean that not all features in iOS 9 are available on each model – for example, Siri can't run on iPad 2.

Above: If there is an update available it will be ready for wireless download and installation from the Software Update area.

Updating Wirelessly

Tap Settings, General, then Software update. This shows the version number and if an update is available. If there is a newer version, follow the on-screen instructions to download and install the update. If your battery is less than half-strength, you'll be warned to connect your iPad to a power source.

Updating via iTunes

Connect your iPad to your Mac or PC and click on your iPad's name in the top menu bar, then the Summary tab. You can see the version and a message stating when iTunes will next automatically check for an update. If you don't want to wait until then, click the Check for Update button. If one is available, follow the instructions to download and install.

BROWSER SETTINGS

While you control the way you browse the web through Safari itself, some of the default settings, such as your search engine of choice, are changed elsewhere.

Changing Safari

Go to Settings and tap Safari in the list on the left-hand side.

Above: Select Safari from the Settings menu to alter your internet browsing settings, such as turning on AutoFill and adjusting how new tabs are opened.

○ **Search engine:** Google is the first choice of most, but you can change this to Yahoo! or Bing.

○ **AutoFill:** repeatedly filling in the same information on web forms is a nuisance. Turn AutoFill on and it will use your info from the Contacts app or other forms you've previously completed. If you turn on Names and Passwords, Safari will remember the username and passwords used to access some websites.

○ **Open New Tabs in Background:** turn this on and when you tap for a new page, it appears in the background while you stay on the page you have open.

○ **Show Favourites Bar:** turn this on and Safari will display the bookmarked sites you have saved as Favourites.

GENERAL SETTINGS

Select General from the list of settings, then About. Tap Name and enter a new one for your iPad. This is used when you connect to iTunes or sync your apps with the computer.

You can also see the Capacity of your iPad, while Available shows how much space you have left. This section also lists how many songs, videos, photos and apps you have stored.

App Settings

Most apps downloaded from the App Store have settings that you can change to customize the way they work. Typically, these are applied within the app itself. There are other, more general settings,

Above: Select General from the Settings menu to enter a name for your iPad and view its remaining space capacity.

which apply to an app, that are controlled through the iPad's Settings app.

1. Tap the Settings app on the Home screen. On the left, underneath the list of built-in apps, are the other apps that have additional settings.

2. Tap them to see what's available. Some of them have very little information – for example, the BBC iPlayer simply gives a version number.

3. Others offer a much more extensive range of settings to change. With Hootsuite, for example, you can change font size, the number of messages to load as well as where to save photos.

4. Once you have changed a setting, tap the button at the top to return to the previous screen.

Hot Tip

Even though your iPad is described as 16GB, 32GB, 64GB, 128GB and 256GB the Capacity shown is always less. For example, a 64GB shows as 57.2GB. The difference is taken up by the operating system and other files that make your iPad work.

TROUBLESHOOTING

While most problems on the iPad are easily resolved, there are times when you'll have to dig a little deeper to get the best performance and keep it running smoothly.

CONNECTIVITY

For most people Wi-Fi is the main way they connect the iPad to their home network. When it goes wrong, there are a series of steps to take to try to sort the problem.

Wireless

Check initially that the problems aren't with your Wi-Fi network. The easiest way is to see if other devices are able to connect and working properly. If they're not, restarting your router might sort out the glitch. If the problem is just on the iPad, try the following.

○ **Turning on Airplane mode:** tap Settings then switch the button beside Airplane Mode to On. After a few seconds turn it Off. This will force the iPad to quit the network and try to reconnect.

○ **Restarting Wi-Fi:** tap Settings, then Wi-Fi, select the network you were connected to and tap the Renew Lease button.

○ **Re-entering the network settings:** follow the same path as the restart but this time tap Forget this Network. Then hard reset the iPad by holding down the Home button and Wake/Sleep button

Above: Restart your Wi-Fi by tapping Renew Lease or Forget this Network and then resetting the iPad.

together until the iPad restarts and the Apple icon appears. Tap Settings, Wi-Fi and re-enter your network settings.

○ **Resetting the network**: Go to Settings, tap General, then Reset and press the Reset Network Settings button.

SYNC PROBLEMS

Given the complexity of the task, there are surprisingly few problems with syncing your iPad – and those there are can be quickly resolved.

Syncing New Apps

Great: you've bought the latest version of a killer game or fantastic app from iTunes, but it isn't syncing with the iPad. What to do?

○ **Make sure you're running the latest version of iOS**: some apps can run only on the most advanced version of the operating system. To see if an upgrade is available, go to Settings, General, then Software Update.

○ **Look to see if you have enough space**: particularly if there's an error message in iTunes

Above: If an app isn't syncing properly it may be a space issue, use iTunes to check how much space is left on your iPad.

or the app isn't fully downloaded during a Wi-Fi sync (the app's icon will appear dimmed on the screen and the progress bar will be blank).

- **Make space for new apps:** apps are compressed for downloading and then expanded during installation, so even if you have space to download the app, there may not be room for the full app. Back up your iPad, then try deleting similarly sized apps and try again.

> **Hot Tip**
>
> TV shows and movies will probably take up the most space on your iPad. Rather than download them, stream them from your computer to your iPad using Home Sharing.

Ghost Apps

These sometimes appear when syncing goes wrong – especially over Wi-Fi. The app's icon will appear on screen dimmed, but when you try and launch the app, nothing happens.

- **Delete the app on your iPad:** tap-and-hold the icon until all apps start to jiggle, then press the delete button.

- **Delete the app in iTunes:** if the above doesn't work, connect your iPad to your computer, select it in iTunes and click on the Apps tab. Scroll to the Home screen where the app is and delete it, then click Apply to sync with your iPad.

- **Do a hard reset:** press the Home button and Wake/Sleep button on the top together and keep holding them until the Apple logo appears on the iPad to show it has restarted.

Sync Problems with iTunes

Syncing by Wi-Fi or cable with iTunes is very convenient, until you find that your iPad appears to have vanished.

- **Syncing by Wi-Fi**: it may be a simple problem of the network having crashed momentarily. Switch Wi-Fi off and on on the iPad by going to Settings and toggling Airplane Mode on then off. You may also have to relaunch the Wi-Fi connection on your Mac or PC.

- **Restarts**: first try closing and then re-opening iTunes on your Mac or PC. If this doesn't work, restart your iPad and Mac or PC.

Above: If your internet crashes, you can toggle Airplane Mode on then off in your Wi-Fi settings to reconnect it quickly.

- **Syncing by cable**: also check you are using the right cable (the iPhone charger cable is very similar but doesn't carry the same power) and try a different USB port to see if that makes any difference.

Sync Problems with iCloud

Although we are used to everything happening quickly, details you enter in your calendar or new bookmarks aren't synchronized instantly. You should only worry that there's a problem if nothing is syncing.

- **Are you on the same network?**: make sure that you are using the same Wi-Fi network and account details for iCloud on your Mac and iPad. If necessary, try deleting and re-entering the information.

- **Make sure that sharing is enabled**: on the iPad go to Settings, iCloud, then Account. You should also check that the various services – Mail, Contacts, Calendar, etc. – are turned on and set to sync.

iPAD BEHAVING BADLY

Sometimes, even the very best things go wrong: when the iPad freezes, apps crash or are not performing, try these steps, which are progressively more severe, to resolve the issue.

○ **Quit the app**: if an app freezes or refuses to do as you want, try closing it down completely. To do this, double-press the Home button to open up the multitasking bar, then swipe up to remove the app's preview screen. This shuts down the app.

○ **Force the App to Shut Down**: if the app refuses to leave quietly, you'll have to make it. To force quit hold the Sleep/Wake button at the top for a few seconds until the Power-Off slider appears. Now hold the Home button for about the same time – 10 seconds – and you'll be back on the main Home screen, but the app that was open will have closed.

Above: If an app crashes double-click the Home button to get to the multitasking bar. Swipe to close down the app.

Above: Search for lost apps using the Spotlight bar which can be found by swiping down from the top of any of your Home Screens.

○ **Restart iPad**: as with many an electrical device, simply turning the iPad off and then on again can do wonders. Hold down the Sleep/Wake button at the top and when the Power-Off slider appears, slide it across to shut down the iPad. Press the Sleep/Wake button again to restart the iPad.

○ **Reset iPad**: this clears most problems. Press-and-hold the Home button at the same time as the Sleep/Wake button at the top and continue to do so until the iPad restarts and the Apple icon appears.

○ **Restore iPad**: whatever has gone wrong, now you can try to get round it by rolling back to the most recent backup you have for the iPad. Connect the iPad to your Mac or PC, select it from the top menu bar in iTunes and then press the Summary tab. Click Restore iPad. Select the most recent backup to restore your software and settings.

○ **Recovery mode**: if Restore fails to complete, the iPad stops responding or continually restarts but never reaches the Home screen, then this is the ultimate step.

1. Connect the USB cable to your computer's USB port but don't yet attach it to the iPad.

2. Turn off the iPad the normal way. If it doesn't turn off, press and hold the Home button and Sleep/Wake button until it does.

3. Press and hold the Home button and connect the iPad to the USB cable. Continue to hold until you get a Connect to iTunes screen.

4. Release the Home button and open iTunes. You should see a message that it is in recovery mode. All your content on the iPad will be erased but once it has been recovered you can restore your settings from a previous backup in the normal way.

Hot Tip

Help! Can't find a new app? There's room on your iPad for 11 pages – Home Screens – full of apps. After that the apps will be there but the only way of finding them is to use Spotlight and search by name. Longer term, think of rearranging your apps in folders.

Above: Search for lost apps using the Spotlight bar which can be found by swiping to the right of your Home Screens.

POWER

You can do so much with your iPad, but as you do more, you do put pressure on the battery. There are ways to conserve power, so you have the energy you need.

Charging Tips

With early versions of the iPad you could plug the device in and use it while it recharged. Since the third generation iPad, this makes the recharge several hours longer.

> ## Hot Tip
>
> **Strangely, fully charging your iPad and then using it until the power's right down is a good way of improving battery performance. You should try to do this at least once a month.**

○ **Recharge the battery**: the best way to recharge the battery is to use the Apple-supplied power adapter to connect the iPad to a power source and turn the device off or put it in sleep mode.

○ **Drained battery**: an empty battery doesn't have enough power to show the Home screen, so if your iPad screen is blank when you turn it on, it may have no battery charge. Plug it in and within a few minutes you should see the Charging Please Wait screen. It will be about 10 minutes before there's enough power to see the Home screen.

Above: Battery in Settings shows the proportion of battery used by each app in the last 24 hours.

○ **iPad USB connector**: only use the iPad USB connector, although others, such as the one for the iPhone, look similar, they are not powerful enough to charge the iPad.

○ **Not Charging**: you may see the message Not Charging on the iPad status bar, typically, this is when you're trying to charge the iPad through the USB port on your computer. Some older machines don't supply enough power to charge the iPad this way.

○ **Battery percentage indicator**: turn this on so you can see how much charge you have left. Tap Settings, General, Usage, then turn on Battery Percentage.

○ **Battery Usage**: also under the battery settings you can see how much power individual apps have taken over the last 24 hours and shutdown the energy-guzzlers. You can also see usage since your last full charge.

Saving Power

Some features consume more battery power than others and you can conserve energy by turning them off when they're not in use.

○ **Sleep mode:** is the ultimate way of saving power when the iPad is not in use. Activate it by pressing the Sleep/Wake button at the top of the iPad.

○ **Alter screen brightness**: tap Settings, then Display & Brightness and move the slider to the left.

○ **Turn off Wi-Fi and Cellular**: as your iPad will always try to maintain a connection to a network, you may want to turn these off when you're in areas with low or limited coverage. Go to Settings, Wi-Fi and turn Wi-Fi off. For mobile go to Settings, Cellular and turn off Cellular Data.

○ **Minimize location services**: such as Maps, which can rapidly reduce battery

Above: Turning off location services you are not using will make your iPad battery last for longer.

life. Go to Settings, Privacy and turn off the Location Services you don't want.

○ **Switch off push notifications**: some apps are constantly checking when new data is available and will send an alert – push notification – when it is. To disable this, go to Settings, Notifications and turn off Notifications. Similarly, turn off Push Mail when you don't need it or don't want to be disturbed by it. Go to Settings, Mail, Contacts, Calendars, Fetch New Data and set Push to off.

Above: Turn off Push mail notifications and change the Fetch frequency to Manually to stop the app gathering new data so often, thus saving battery.

○ **Fetch data less frequently**: instead of having them push new messages to you, you can get applications such as Mail to fetch new data wirelessly after a specific time interval. The shorter the interval, the more frequently data is fetched and the quicker the drain on your battery. Save power by turning this to Manual – Settings, Mail, Contacts, Calendars, Fetch New Data and tap Manually – or setting the Fetch period to a longer time interval, such as hourly.

Hot Tip

While you can lower screen brightness through the Settings app as above, iBooks has its own brightness control which lets you dim the screen even more.

RUNNING OUT OF SPACE

Even at 64GB to 256GB the larger capacity iPads don't offer much storage space compared with a computer. With new apps doing more, they are becoming larger and it's very easy to fill the available space on your iPad quickly.

Managing Storage Space

If you are running low on storage, there's a quick way of finding out what apps are using the most space, so you can delete those you don't use often.

1. Tap Settings, General, Storage & iCloud Usage then Manage Storage. It may take a little time, while it calculates, but eventually the iPad lists your apps and the amount of space each one takes. Tap an individual app, such as Videos, and you'll get a breakdown of the size occupied by TV series plus individual movies and clips.

2. For most apps, the app itself takes up little space. Most of the storage is for documents and data it stores, such as photos, videos, music, large documents and the like. Before deleting an app completely, it's worth opening it up to see if it contains files that you could delete to save space.

Above: You can check how much storage space individual apps are taking up by tapping Settings, General, Storage & iCloud Usage, then Manage Storage. Free up space by deleting those apps which you don't use very often.

3. Tap the Usage button to return to the previous screen and then Show all Apps to see a full list of the size of each app. The more apps you have, the longer it takes to build the list.

4. With this information it's easier to clear space. If you decide to delete the biggest apps that you don't use: tap on the app then press Delete App.

Hot Tip

Not all apps can be deleted, including those built into iOS, such as the Photos & Camera app or the Music app, which fortunately means you can't accidentally delete all your photos or songs.

ACCESSORIZING

There are accessories for your iPad that enhance its look, protect it from everyday knocks or, like the wireless keyboard, extend the way it works to make it even easier to use.

COVERS

From the colourful and zany to the highly functional smart covers, there's plenty of choice when it comes to cases for your iPad. Search online if you are interested in purchasing any of the accessories that follow.

Smart Cover

Through a series of magnets Apple's smart cover sticks to the side of the iPad. Another set of magnets attach it to the screen, so that opening the cover wakes up the device and closing it puts the iPad to sleep. Inside the micro-fibre surface helps keep the screen clean. The cover also folds into a triangle to create a small stand for the iPad. This is suitable for the iPad 2 and above.

Leather Portfolio

Go eco-friendly but stay smart with these recycled leather cases for the iPad, which also double as stands. Find the Proporta Recycled Leather Eco Case at www.proporta.com/smart.

Paper Sleeve

What makes this different is the fact that you can

Above: The Papernomad iPad sleeve.

doodle your own designs on the tear-resistant paper cover, while the inside cushioning of cotton and wool protects the iPad. Find the sleeve at www.papernomad.com.

BookBook

Should you want to disguise the ultimate modern tablet as a vintage book, these leather hardback cases are for you. They also double up as a typing and display stand and some have slots for your credit and debit cards.

STANDS

If you don't want to cover up the elegance of the iPad itself, go for a stand which lets you view the screen hands-free, even watch videos in bed or attach it to a microphone stand for making a speech or presentation.

PadFoot

A remarkably simple but stylish idea, the PadFoot just clips to the corner of your iPad. It can be used in both landscape and portrait mode. Small enough to be carried easily, it's convenient for use with a wireless keyboard, or standing up the iPad for in-store displays and meeting presentations. Find the PadFoot at www.michielcornelissen.com/padfoot_stand_for_ipad.html.

Hover Bar

This attaches to any iMac or Apple Display with an L-shaped desk stand and lets you have your iPad beside the big screen, so you can keep an eye on Twitter, the weather or have a FaceTime chat. If you don't have a Mac, the simple silicone-lined clamp makes it easy to set up the

Left: The PadFoot clips to the corner of your iPad and keeps it upright without you having to hold it.

iPad for viewing in the kitchen or other room. Find the Hover Bar at www.twelvesouth.com.

Swingholder

This is designed to keep the iPad at eye-level, whether you're on a treadmill in the gym, lying down in bed or standing on a stage. Based on a microphone stand, it has a weighted base and adjustable swing arm. However it is relatively expensive compared to other stands. Find the Swingholder on Amazon.

SOUND

Share the music on your iPad at a family get together or in the office by streaming it wirelessly to an external speaker or listen through your headphones to songs playing on the iPad in your backpack.

Wireless Speakers

As portable as your iPad, the JBL Flip can stream music wirelessly from any Bluetooth-equipped iPad, while the more expensive Bose SoundLink uses Apple's wireless technology AirPlay for what the manufacturers state is clear, room-filling music. Find these speakers at the Apple Store.

Right: The JBL flip speakers can be used to wirelessly stream music from your iPad if the Bluetooth is enabled.

Headphones

No wires needed with Bluetooth-connected headphones, like these ones from Logitech. As most manufacturers offer Bluetooth-enabled headsets that would work with the iPad, make your choice on comfort, sound quality and reliability. Find these headphones at the Apple Store.

INPUTS

While the iPad's touch screen is great for writing email and such, for longer pieces of text a proper keyboard is much faster and more convenient. And if you want more precise handwritten text or drawings, there are iPad pens to help.

Above: The Logitech UE headphones are Bluetooth-enabled, allowing for easy wireless access to the music stored on your iPad.

Keyboard Stand

This dock has a keyboard physically attached, so you can type – as well as sync, charge and more. Special keys provide quick access to iPad features you use often, such as the Home screen, search and the screen lock. Find the keyboard dock at stores, including John Lewis.

Smart Keyboard

Designed for the iPad Pro, it acts as a full-size keyboard when needed or slim lightweight cover. It is powered by the Smart Connector on the iPad Pro which allows for a two-way exchange of power and data.

Bluetooth Keyboard

More traditional keyboards use Bluetooth. This is a short-range wireless technology that will connect two devices up to about 30 feet away. Because it doesn't need a line of sight connection, it works well with headsets, speakers and particularly keyboards.

- **Apple:** offer a wireless keyboard, which works with Macs too. Slim and compact, it takes up about a quarter less space than the normal full-sized keyboard. Battery-powered, it will switch off automatically to save power when you're not using the keyboard and then restart instantly when you start typing again. Find the keyboard at the Apple Store.

Above: The iPad Keyboard acts as both a dock for your iPad and a battery-powered wireless keyboard.

○ **Kensington:** are among several manufacturers who provide the ultimate iPad travel pack with a case that doubles as a stand and a Bluetooth-enabled keyboard. There are compatible versions available for each iPad generation. Find the keyboard and folio case at www.kensington.com.

Apple Pencil

The iPad Pro series also saw the introduction of the Apple Pencil. It allows greater precision for intricate drawings and enables you to annotate or sketch in a variety of apps, such as Notes. Alternatively, the Cosmonaut is a crayon-sized stylus, with a large rubber barrel, that feels like a marker pen but is great for sketching out ideas. Find the Cosmonaut at www.studioneat.com.

Hot Tip

Extend the usefulness of your iPad's cameras with Photojojo's fish eye, wide angle and telephoto lenses that attach by a magnetic ring (photojojo.com).

Above: The Apple Pencil has been introduced with the iPad Pro series.

Widgets	Notifications

Batteries

iPad   100%

Apple Pencil   16%

Accessories

No Favorites

Above: To check on the battery status of your iPad and Apple Pencil, you can use the new Battery widget on your iPhone or iPad. Just swipe down from top of your screen to view the Notification Center.

SECURITY

Given the range of all that you can do on the iPad, from your accounts to buying and selling on the web, there are a number of security measures that can help you keep your private information confidential.

PASSWORD PROTECTION

The simplest way of keeping your information private is to use password protection – but there are varying degrees of security to the passcodes you use.

Locking Your iPad – Step-by-Step

1. Go to Settings, then Touch ID & Passcode or just Passcode if you don't have a device with Touch ID.

2. Tap Turn Passcode On and you'll be requested to enter a 6-digit number you'll remember and re-enter it when prompted. If you want to change back to the four-digit number used on iPads before click Passcode, enter your existing passcode then Change Passcode and select Passcode Options. Here you can create your own custom code.

Above: Turn on the passcode option within the general settings menu to increase iPad security.

3. Select Require Passcode and select the interval, from more than four hours to immediately, before the iPad locks. The shorter the interval, the more secure it is.

4. Even when the iPad is locked, there may be certain services you want to use, such as asking Siri to set a Reminder.

Under the Allow Access When Locked section, choose which apps you want to be available in the background.

5. Some iPads come with Touch ID which enables them to open the iPad using Fingerprint recognition. You can change it and your passcode by going to General, then Touch ID & Passcode.

Auto-Lock

You can automatically lock your iPad or turn off the display when it's not in use. Go to Settings, General then Auto-Lock and select the time delay before it switches off, which varies from 15 minutes to 2 minutes. Set to Never if you don't want the iPad to turn off.

Cover Locks

The smart covers available on second generation iPads and later will automatically lock your device when you close the cover and turn it back on when you open the flap.

Encrypting iPad Backups

If you choose this option, passwords for different accounts, such as Mail, will be stored and you won't need to re-enter them individually if you have to use the backup to restore the iPad. Instead, there's one master password you need to restore the backup. To encrypt your backups go to iTunes, select the iPad from the top menu bar, then the Summary tab and check Encrypt iPad Backup.

Hot Tip

You can also lock the iPad or turn off the display manually, at any time, by pressing the Wake/Sleep button at the top of the iPad.

Above: Turn on Smart Cover lock to automatically lock your iPad when you close the cover, and turn it back on when you open it.

iCloud Security

When your personal information is sent from your iPad to iCloud over the internet, it is encrypted, employing the same level of security as that used by major banks. It is also stored on Apple's servers in an encrypted format. That way, your data is kept private and protected from unauthorized access while it's being transmitted to your iPad and when it's stored on iCloud. Apple also recommend you use a strong password with your Apple ID that is used for accessing iCloud. It should be a minimum of eight characters and include uppercase and lowercase letters, and a number.

FIND MY iPAD

Whether your iPad has been stolen or you've simply mislaid it, you can track it down, provided you've already set up Find My iPad.

Find Your Device

1. To start tracking of your iPad, go to Settings, iCloud and turn on Find My iPad.

2. As soon as you've done this, a permission box opens, asking you to confirm you are happy for the iPad to be tracked and its location shown on a map. Tap Allow.

Above: Turn on Find My iPad in your iCloud settings to ensure it can be tracked via Location Services.

3. In Settings tap Privacy and turn on Location Services. Find My iPad should also be turned on.

4. You can download the Find My iPad app (called Find My iPhone) from iTunes and use this on another iDevice, such as iPhone, to track your iPad. Once it's downloaded, log in using your iCloud username and password.

5.   Alternatively, you can log in direct through Find My iPhone on the iCloud website. Go to www.icloud.com and use your Apple ID to sign in. Click on Devices, and any that can be found are shown with a green pin on the map. Any that can't be located will have a red pin.

6.   Click on the pin, and it shows you the last time the iPad was tracked to that address. Click on the information button and a new window opens.

Other features of Find My iPad include:

○ **Play Sound:** sends a strange bell-clanging noise to your iPad – handy if you know it's in your home somewhere, but you have misplaced it.

○ **Lost mode:** lets you lock your iPad remotely, with a four-digit passcode if you haven't set one already, which is useful if you've left it at work or a friend's house.

Above: You can choose actions for when your iPad has been tracked, for example playing sounds, locking it remotely and erasing its content.

○ **Erase iPad:** the nuclear option if you believe it has been stolen, this wipes out all the iPad's content, including your private, sensitive information and restores the device to the original factory settings.

LIMITING ACCESS

If you don't want every user to have full reign over your iPad, such as a business colleague

> ### Hot Tip
> For Find My iPad to work, it has to be turned on at all times, which will use some battery power, but it does offer great peace of mind in case anything happens to your iPad.

or your children, you can limit the areas they can access.

Setting Restrictions

In order to set up the rules of who can access what, tap Settings, General, Restrictions then Enable Restrictions. In the pop-up window set a passcode and re-enter to confirm.

Above: Set up restrictions to limit access to parts of your iPad.

○ **Restrict Apps:** If you turn off any of the apps listed here – which include Safari, Camera and apps that use it, FaceTime, iTunes Store, iBookstore and Siri – they can only be used by someone who knows the password.

○ **Disable Installing of Apps:** the App Store is also disabled and its icon is removed from the Home screen. Alternatively, if you keep the App Store accessible, you can prevent your children from adding expensive extras to apps by turning off In-App Purchases or Require a Password before they can buy.

○ **Prevent Deleting of Apps:** by removing the delete icon (x) from the corner of apps.

○ **Avoid Explicit Language:** with Siri using asterisks and beep sounds to cover any unfortunate words that may slip out during dictation.

○ **Lock your accounts:** including your current Mail, Contacts, Calendar and iCloud settings.

○ **Set Content Restrictions:** for music and podcasts, books, movies, TV shows, and apps, according to the country you select from the list. Any content outside of the ratings you select won't be shown on the iPad.

Above: Turn on Guided Access to use kiosk mode to limit your iPad to a single app when needed.

Guided Access

If you want to share a single presentation, use your iPad solely as a photo frame during a party or have your child focus on a single game, then you can use kiosk mode. This limits the iPad to a single app, with you controlling what features are available.

Tap Settings, then General, Accessibility, Guided Access and slide the button to On. Set a passcode to use. Select the app you want to use, triple-press the Home button, adjust the settings and press Start.

PRIVACY SETTINGS

You can control which apps have access to your personal information in your contacts, calendars, reminders and photos, as well as Twitter and Facebook.

Controlling Access

The first time an app tries to access your personal information, a pop-up box will ask if you allow this or not. Whatever your response, the decision stands and the app won't ask again. However, you can change your mind.

To change your privacy choice, go to Settings, Privacy and select one of the apps from the list, for example Contacts. Here you'll see a list of apps, such as Skype or Find Friends, that have asked to access this personal information. You can allow or disallow access by switching the button to On or Off.

Hot Tip

If you want to wipe the slate clean and start again, you can reset all your privacy warnings. Go to Settings, General, Reset and tap Reset Location & Privacy.

Above: Activate the Limit Ad Tracking setting to prevent online advertisers from using your web data to target you specifically.

Stop Ad Tracking

This prevents advertisers using your web usage data and cookies (which have information about the sites you visit) to target specific ads to you.

To turn it on go to Settings, Privacy and s croll down to Advertising, then turn on Limit Ad Tracking.

Fraud Warning

Go to Settings, Safari and scroll down to turn this on. This checks websites you visit against a public database of problem sites. If you follow a link to one of these sites, you get a warning, so you can stop loading the page.

VPN

Connect securely and privately to your office network, via the internet, using a virtual private network (VPN).

Hot Tip

You can have more than one VPN connection and switch between them on the VPN settings page. A VPN button appears in the status bar when you're using the secure connection.

Setting up a VPN Connection

Go to the Settings app, select VPN and and then Add VPN Configuration.

In the window that opens enter your network settings, which you will need to get from your IT department (or copy from your Mac or PC if you already have a VPN set up on your computer). When complete, tap Save.

APPTASTIC: 100 BEST iPAD APPS

There are more than a quarter of a million apps designed exclusively for the iPad in the App Store. Many are brilliant, some not so. Here, in line with the different categories covered in this book, is our pick of the essential apps (excluding built-in apps) for a fantastic iPad experience.

Communication

1. **Facebook**: The official app for the world's largest social network.

2. **Friendly for Facebook**: The full Facebook experience designed specifically for the iPad.

3. **Twitter**: All you need to go a-tweeting.

4. **Tweetbot**: Nice design and lots of ways to customize your Twitter experience.

5. **LinkedIn**: Keep in touch with your professional network.

6. **HootSuite for Twitter and Facebook**: Manage several of your social networks from one app.

7. **StumbleUpon**: Stumble your way through a creative network of videos, photos and web pages.

8. **Skype for iPad**: Instant message, voice or video call to friends and family around the world.

9. **Find My Friends**: Stalk your friends and family.

10. **Google Maps**: Once powered the built-in Maps app but now there's only this iPhone version for the iPad.

Connectivity

11. **iTap VNC (Remote Desktop for Windows and Mac)**: Manage your desktop from your iPad.

Photos

12. **Guardian Eyewitness**: Daily showcase of some of the most striking and beautiful photographs.

13. **iPhoto**: Browse, edit and share your photos from the iPad.

14. **Adobe Photoshop Touch**: Tablet-designed version of the famous photo-editing software.

15. **Snapseed**: Makes pro-level photo-editing easy.

16. **Brushes 3**: The painting app that's so good that artist David Hockney uses it.

17. **Instagram**: iPhone version of the fun social network for taking and sharing photos.

18. **Instant**: Polaroid instant photos for the iPad.

19. **ComicBook**: Fully featured app for creating comic books.

20. **PhotoSync**: Wirelessly transfers your photos and videos.

21. **Web Albums HD for Picasa and Google+**: Viewer and photo manager for the online photo services.

22. **FlickStackr**: Lets you browse, upload and share photos on Flickr.

23. **eBook Magic**: The app for creating and sharing many types of book.

24. **Greetings Studio**: Easy-to-use greeting card app for the iPad.

25. **InstaCalendar for iPad**: Convenient way of using your photos to create a calendar.

26. **Jigsawed Jigsaw Puzzle**: Easily customizable jigsaw puzzle creator.

TV, Movies and Music Video

27. **YouTube**: No longer a built-in app, but you can still get access to one of the world's greatest collections of videos.

28. **Vimeo**: Designed for watching, creating and sharing videos on the Vimeo site.

29. **iMovie**: Movie-editing for the touchscreen.

30. **Skyfire Web Browser for iPad**: The browser that does let you watch Flash videos on the iPad.

31. **Netflix**: The subscription service for watching TV and films on your iPad.

32. **Matcha – Find and Watch Movies & TV**: Personalized guide for video services.

33. **Plizy**: Discover the best movies, shows and web content online.

34. **Crackle – Movies & TV**: Watch free Hollywood movies and TV shows.

35. **BBC iPlayer**: Watch and listen to BBC TV and Radio.

Books/News

36. **iBooks**: Apple's ebook reader and bookstore.

37. **Google Play Books**: Provides access to millions of books – free and paid-for.

38. **Kindle**: Reader for Kindle books, newspapers, magazines and more from the Amazon store.

39. **Newsweek**: Digital editions especially created for the iPad.

40. **The *Guardian* and *Observer* iPad edition**: The newspapers re-imagined for the iPad.

41. ***MailOnline* for iPad**: Standalone app with customizable international editions linked to the UK's number one newspaper website.

42. **BBC News**: Breaking news from around the world.

43. **Reuters News Pro for iPad**: Professional-grade news and market data.

44. **Early Edition 2**: Edit your own newspaper.

45. **NewsRack**: Fully featured news reader.

46. **Flipboard: Your Social News Magazine**: Personal magazine combining international news sources and your social networks.

47. **Pocket**: Lets you save content from the web to read later.

48. **ESPN ScoreCenter**: Results and news from sports leagues around the world.

49. **Zinio**: Buy and read magazines on your iPad.

50. **Zite**: Personalized magazine that learns what you like.

51. **Comics**: Read comics on your iPad.

52. **Dilbert Mobile**: Animated cartoons on office life.

Reference/Lifestyle

53. **Shakespeare**: The complete works.

54. **Encyclopaedia Britannica**: If you don't trust free encyclopedias, this offers a rolling monthly subscription to one of the most respected reference sources.

55. **Wikipanion**: If you do trust free encyclopedias, this is a faster and easier way to access Wikipedia.

56. **Google Earth**: Fly around the planet from your iPad.

57. **World Atlas HD**: World maps designed specifically to display on the iPad.

58. **Weather**: Is it cold outside? Find out.

59. **HowStuffWorks for iPad**: All you need to know.

60. **NASA App HD**: Explore the universe from your iPad.

61. **National Geographic Magazine-International**: The magazine plus special interactive content.

62. **WebMD**: Health information and symptom checker for the hypochondriac in you.

63. **Epicurious**: Recipes for foodies.

64. **TripAdvisor Hotels Flights Restaurants**: Candid reviews by fellow travellers.

65. **TripDeck**: When you've decided where you're going, this is your itinerary organizer. iPhone app.

66. **Fancy**: Explore and buy from a crowd-created catalogue of amazing gifts and goodies.

Entertainment

67. **Podcasts**: Manage your podcasts.

68. **Spotify**: Access millions of songs and listen free or subscribe.

69. **Last.fm**: iPhone app for access to the music recommendation site from your iPad.

70. **Vevo HD**: High-quality music videos.

71. **TuneIn Radio Pro**: Listen to and record music, sports and news radio around the world.

72. **SoundHound**: Fast music recognition app.

73. **Amazon Cloud Player**: iPhone app for listening to your music stored on the Amazon Cloud.

74. **GarageBand**: Your own recording studio.

75. **Angry Birds**: Destroy greedy pigs in a number of environments.

76. **The Dark Knight Rises**: Game inspired by the movie.

77. **Tiger Woods PGA Tour**: Life as a golf pro.

78. **Scrabble**: The word game designed just for the iPad.

79. **We Rule Deluxe for iPad**: The longest-running social game on iDevices.

Work

80. **GoodReader for iPad**: Robust, flexible PDF reader.

81. **Dictionary.com**: English dictionary and thesaurus for the iPad.

82. **Evernote**: Sync notes, to-do lists, documents, photos and more across all your devices.

83. **Dropbox**: Share and sync your docs, photos and videos.

84. **Things for iPad**: Easy-to-use task manager.

85. **OmniFocus for iPad**: Fully featured organizer for a busy life.

86. **Pages**: Word-processor app for the iPad.

87. **Numbers**: Spreadsheet app for the iPad.

88. **Keynote**: Presentation app for the iPad.

89. **Quickoffice Pro HD**: Edit Microsoft Office documents and view PDF files.

90. **Google Drive**: Create, share and keep all your documents online in one place.

91. **SugarSync**: Online backup, mobile syncing and file sharing.

92. **Blogsy for iPad**: Blog writing for the iPad.

93. **iTranslate**: Translate words and texts into 50 languages.

94. **PrintCentral Pro**: Print to all printers (not just AirPrint printers).

95. **Bento 4 for iPad**: Personal database for organizing contacts, tracking projects and managing lists.

96. **SharePrice**: Track your investments across global markets.

97. **Account Tracker**: Powerful personal finance app.

98. **Countdown Timer Pro**: Build up the anticipation, or anxiety, and count down to any date.

Security

99. **1Password**: Remember the master password and 1Password remembers the rest.

100. **Find My iPhone**: Use another iDevice to find your iPad and protect your data.

INDEX